T0338969

Amazing Diving Stories

Amazing Diving Stories

John Bantin

FERNHURST
BOOKS

This third edition first published in 2021 by Fernhurst Books Limited
The Windmill, Mill Lane, Harbury, Leamington Spa, Warwickshire. CV33 9HP, UK
Tel: +44 (0) 1926 337488 | www.fernhurstbooks.com

First published in hardback in 2012 by John Wiley & Sons Ltd
Published in paperback in 2014 by Fernhurst Books Limited

A catalogue record for this book is available from the British Library
ISBN 978-1-912621-38-5

Cover photo © John Bantin
Cover design: Rachel Atkins & Daniel Stephen

Set in 12/14pt Garamond by Aptara Inc., New Delhi, India
Printed in Bulgaria by Multiprint

CONTENTS

CONTENTS

CONTENTS

INTRODUCTION

The world under water is every bit as complicated as it is on land. However, relatively few people get to witness it. Many dive locations are by necessity in remote and out-of-the-way places. Often it's as much of an adventure to simply get there. Every diver comes back with a story, so there is no shortage. Dive sites and dive boats ring loudly with the anecdotes told, each better than the last. By the very nature of things, most of what happens under water is seen by very few and like fishermen's tales they can get changed or exaggerated. Some of those involved have differing recollections long after the event. More than twenty years as a full-time diving journalist has exposed the author to many strange experiences. All that happened in most of the stories collected here, was witnessed either first-hand or told to him by the protagonists very soon after the event. In some cases, people have preferred to remain anonymous. Many of the stories, or elements of them, first saw the light of day in *Diver* magazine.

PART ONE

Animal Encounters

CLOSE CALL WITH A HUMPBACK WHALE

Rarely will a mother and calf be seen without an escort male that takes responsibility for shepherding the pair safely, but woe betide the diver who dares to annoy the escort with aggressive behaviour.

During his Navy diving days in 1971, Bret Gilliam had worked collecting data from fast attack nuclear submarines. It was in the superb visibility afforded by the waters off the US Virgin Islands. During the long underwater decompression stops required, he had often seen humpback whales. He became an enthusiastic humpback spotter and this eventually led to 20 annual trips to the Silver Banks, an area between the Dominican Republic and Grand Turk. It's now an area well-known among divers for encounters with humpback whales and their young calves.

"Standing on their tails and bobbing in the gentle evening sea, they positioned themselves with their heads turned, to present eyes the size of hockey pucks that seemed to look right through you. At that point, the experience of swimming with our military's subs seemed pretty pale by comparison."

It was common to see pregnant females disappear and reappear a day or so later with a calf in tow, but nobody has ever recorded a mother whale giving birth. Where they go to and how the birth is accomplished, is still one of life's big mysteries.

It was February 1993. The weather was not too good and it was extremely windy. Diving out in the open ocean was out of the question and "for want of anything better to do", Bret left the boat and went alone for a shallow dive in the lee of a coral reef, swimming among the coral pillars that punctuated the sandy bottom. Even here he could not escape the whales' presence, with their haunting songs flowing over and around the underwater landscape and filling his ears as he swam.

He was very surprised indeed to round a coral head and come face to face with a mother whale and her calf. "I was fewer than 3 m (10 ft) from them," he recalled. What an opportunity for an underwater photographer!

The whales were resting with the baby lying under its mother's watchful gaze. It was the smallest calf Bret had ever seen at around only 2 m long (6 ft) and 110 kg (250 lb). In fact, he remembered thinking it was about the same size and weight as him.

"My mind was racing. Was this a newborn calf? Had I nearly stumbled on what every photographer in the world had sought for decades? Certainly, the calf was the right size and clearly was so young that he couldn't hold his breath for more than few seconds. I cradled my camera and began to line up the shots.

Sure enough, the pair were waiting for me as I eased around the massive coral buttress into water that was now barely 5 m (15 ft) deep.

It was surreal to see this leviathan mother some 15 m (50 ft) in length easing herself over the smooth sandy bottom. Her massive pectoral fins gently grazed the sand leaving a trench marking her trail, while the baby rode the pressure wave just above her head. The depth lessened even more and her belly barely cleared the bottom. I moved to the coral head and clung to an outcrop to let them pass, all the while firing away with my wide angle."

As the mother's 6 m (20 ft) tail fluke filled his lens from only inches away, Bret began a slow pursuit but all the while wondering why there was no escort male supervising the pair. Maybe the rambunctious males were simply too cautious of the shallow water that might have stranded them?

Bret was suddenly aware that the bottom was no longer 5 m (15 ft) below him. His fin tips hit something solid when he kicked and he looked down thinking he'd let himself drift onto the coral head.

"Wrong! The male I had been speculating about was directly below me, having been masked in the gloom before. He had now set his sights on moving up to place himself between his new family and me. He had accelerated his slow swim and I now found him about to surface directly between my legs!

To my left were the jagged coral branches of the reef top and Mr Big chose that moment to raise his pectoral fin to just clear the hazard. His fin soared over the coral head like a stunt airplane turning around a course pylon. That effectively killed any escape in that direction. A quick look behind confirmed that the whale's back would make contact with me in seconds. I gulped a breath and dove over his head with my chest massaging his widow's peak on the way by. Finning to give us each some space I ended up about 1 m (3 ft) off the bottom and under his right pectoral fin.

Okay, this isn't so bad, I thought. He'll just glide over me and then I can come up. Wrong again! He chose that exact moment to stop and simultaneously dropped his pectoral fin neatly pinning me to the sand. I had always wanted a close encounter but this was ridiculous. There I was, flat on my back with several tons of deadweight pectoral gently anchoring me. I never even thought of struggling. I lay quietly and played dead. Rather aptly, I thought.

From my constrained view I could look the big guy in the eye from about 1.5 m (5 ft) away. He articulated his gaze back to me and sized me up. After about 30 seconds he eased up his pectoral fin and moved ahead. I put one hand up and fended myself off his belly as he moved over me at a snail's pace. Finally, the tail passed overhead and close enough to let me count the smallest barnacles. I gratefully hit the surface for some much needed air.

While I was taking an inventory of my own body parts and mentally calculating if I qualified for hypoxia-induced brain damage, all three whales came at me from the shallows. The male led the mother and her baby deftly through the reef and then waited for them to exit to the deeper water. We regarded each other without malice as he ended up once again on the surface right next to me. I fired off a few frames and then he moved gradually away into the blue with his charges."

WHITE-TIPS AT NIGHT

Often described as "inoffensive" and "not aggressive", white-tip reef sharks are the species of shark most often encountered by divers and probably the least often written about.

Night-time at Manuelita Rock. It was dark, very dark. Richard Skepper lowered himself quietly into the inky black water with his video camera safe inside its marine housing. At what seemed to be a very long way below him, he could see a dim green glow. He dropped through emptiness, slowly rotating round as he went. The beams of his video lamps picked up nothing but plankton and the occasional jellyfish, and although powerful, were blocked by the foggy underwater conditions. No fish were evident.

He headed towards that green glow. As he got closer he could see it was the light of another diver who had entered the water before him. He was hovering over a seabed of coral rubble, rocks and sand and looking at a large green turtle that he had disturbed from its slumbers. It stared back, bleary eyed, into the beam of his light. It was lying on the sand, not moving.

Both divers then became aware that all around them were hundreds of pairs of white eyes, glinting hungrily from the darkness. A pack of wolves? No, these were the subaquatic equivalent – hordes of sharks, revving up for a night of frantic hunting. Something was about to die!

No wonder all the fish had gone into hiding. This was not a safe place for the small and vulnerable. Only a few large, evil-looking black jacks flitted excitedly in and out of their lamp beams. It seemed that they were goading the sharks into action in the hope of picking off some unfortunate prey that might escape the throng.

The lights attracted other animals now. An eagle ray almost crashed into them. It was like a cross between some giant demented moth and a creature from Harry Potter. More than a metre (3 ft) wide, the divers got a flash of its white underbody and black top with spots. It flapped its wings and returned into the darkness as quickly as it came.

The two divers swam slowly together at 18 m (58 ft) deep. The seabed below them quickly cluttered up with grey cigar shapes. The sharks seemed to be taking advantage of their lights. It became a crazy cross between the Pied Piper and two huntsmen whipping in the hounds. But were the divers leading or were they being led? These wolves were on a mission.

More sharks joined the hunt. They hugged the bottom, checking every cluster of rocks. No hiding place went unexamined. The seabed, now lit in joint pools of light, was solid with grey bodies, purposefully moving as one, and with one intention – the destruction of the weak and ill, and any small creature unfortunate enough to cross their path.

How many sharks were there? Fifty? One hundred? Two hundred? More?

The occasional marble ray, a not inconsequential animal, hugged the sand closely as the horde passed over. Lobsters scuttled quickly back into their holes. The night belonged to the sharks, their white eyes glinting. Then it happened.

Something must have revealed certain vulnerability. A shark darted after it, into a hole. Another followed. Then there was the scrum. The scrum was without rules. It was a scrum that was a tussle of 50 animals trying to get into one small crevice. It was a scrum that bit and gouged and writhed desperately to deliver death. No longer wolves hunting, it had become a snake pit of slender grey bodies, a grim demonstration of unyielding determination. The mob ruled.

Richard hovered over it with his camera at the ready. Only a couple of feet above the action, he made sure he didn't sink any lower. These animals may not be man-eaters but at this moment they would bite anything that moved, including a hand accidentally extended to steady on the rock below. The fight went on.

Remarkably, a large lobster escaped unscathed but not unruffled from the intended carnage. It darted to another hideaway. Richard recorded about 30 minutes of this action, his video lamps lighting up the affray, a turmoil of thrashing tails and boiling sand. The sharks were not distracted from their mission. It was a mission to eat whatever revealed the weakness that denoted its role – that of the prey.

Then one shark escaped with the remains of a small red fish hanging from its mouth. It made a dash away into deeper water. There was a brief lull as some sharks gave chase and the hunt resumed. The divers swam onwards, their lamps lighting up the seabed, solid with grey cigar-shaped bodies, purposefully moving as one, and with one intention . . .

Richard had travelled to the lonely outpost of Cocos Island, which lies 350 miles from the coast of Costa Rica in the Pacific, to video the hammerhead sharks that were known to school there. Cocos was used as the island from which King Kong was captured in the original movie. It prompted Robert Louis Stevenson to write *Treasure Island* and Michael Crichton to write *Jurassic Park*.

It was not the hammerhead sharks that revealed to Richard nature red in tooth and jaw. It was the little white-tip reef sharks.

Usually seen singly or in small groups in daytime, resting on the bottom while they pump water through their gills (something few other sharks can do), they can be recognised easily by the large white tip on their first dorsal fin and the upper lobe of the tail. They mature at 1 m (3 ft) in length but can vary in size from a couple of feet to more than 2 m (6 ft). They are very flexible in movement and are almost able to turn back on themselves and touch their tails. They have tough skins, which allow them to squeeze into small openings and hunt aggressively among the rocks and coral. They can be encountered in large numbers hunting at night in places such as Maya Thilla in the Maldives and Sipadan Island, but nowhere can they be seen in such grotesque numbers as Cocos Island, in the eastern Pacific.

They eat a wide range of prey, often octopus and small molluscs. They are not normally considered dangerous to man but they hunt at night, every night. For Richard, it was a dive that he would never forget.

LORD TEBBIT AND THE TURTLE

Lord Norman Tebbit learns to dive and gets injured in the process.

Norman Tebbit was first a flyer with the RAF. He distinguished himself by walking away from his burning Meteor aircraft after crashing it on take-off from RAF Waterheath. He then went on to become a pilot and navigator with the airline BOAC and took a prominent role with the British pilots' union, BALPA. Away from work, he became involved in politics. After being elected as a Member of Parliament in 1970, he became one of Margaret Thatcher's right-hand men.

After a career in which he was blown up by Sinn Fein/IRA in the Grand Hotel in Brighton, and broke the power of the coalminers' union led by Arthur Scargill, he was elevated to the House of Lords as Baron Tebbit and made a Companion of Honour. He had become a legitimate member of "the great and the good".

During this later time, he took to writing a column in the *Mail on Sunday* and on one occasion he reported his experiences of white-water rafting in Colorado.

"Goodness me," he wrote, "I'll be taking up scuba diving next!"

The owner of *Diver* magazine in the UK immediately invited him to learn to dive and at the age of 68, he became the subject of a feature in that magazine. Eventually, Lord Tebbit's own written feature resulting from this experience made three whole pages in the *Daily Mail*. It was entitled "The day my life turned turtle".

He wrote, "Diving is not like swimming. It is more like flying, more like being in a small airship able to adjust buoyancy to stabilise at any chosen depth."

His diving instructor recalls, "Lord Tebbit was easy to teach because you dive with your brain rather than your muscles. However, I was ever aware of the enormous responsibility for my trainee and didn't want to achieve what the IRA had failed to do. I was very careful with this very important gentleman."

After initial pool training in the UK, they travelled together with Lady Margaret Tebbit to Barbados in order to make those initial open-water dives in easy and benign conditions.

"He seemed a little frail and I was scared stiff that he might get injured jumping for the first time from a boat while carrying heavy diving equipment, so for that first dip into the sea I chose to walk with him into the water from the safety of a beach close to our hotel."

It wasn't a regular dive site and as soon as they were submerged, the instructor started to regret his decision. There seemed to be absolutely nothing to look at apart from a few mooring blocks for some boats and acres and acres of boring-looking sand as far as the eye could see. One of the most important aspects of a novice diver's first sea dive is to make all the effort seem worthwhile.

Here the report from the great man seems to conflict with that of the younger instructor's contemporaneous magazine article. Lord Tebbit recounts it as his second dive when in fact it was his first trip out into the sea.

Notwithstanding that, the instructor remembers struggling to find anything interesting to show his lordship until, as luck would have it, two large green turtles appeared out of nowhere. Not only that, but they swam directly towards the two divers and the instructor readied his underwater camera in the hope of getting a turtle in the same shot as the British baron. A close encounter with a green turtle in Barbados is a very rare event indeed. What neither man knew was that these turtles had originally been rescued from fishermen when small, and regularly hand fed by locals, so consequently had little fear of humans. This was unusual.

Lord Tebbit continued in his own article, "Imagine something the size of a small sheep flying around your head, pushing and shoving as it importuned for food, and you have got the idea. Nobody told me that turtles are greedy, have poor eyesight and sharp beaks. Being a little slow to react I finished up streaming blood from a bitten finger, my only diving injury so far – and subject of great hilarity to my companion."

The instructor had mixed feelings. First, he had recorded some marvellous close-up pictures of a peer of the realm in the close company of a green turtle, with which he was elated; but at the same time his responsibility to keep this important gentleman safe from harm seemed to have been jeopardised within the first minutes of being in the water. Later, he discovered he had recorded the very moment of the bite and this was reproduced at nearly full-page size accompanying his lordship's newspaper feature. Thankfully, the great man took it in good humour and spent the rest of the trip enjoying less eventful experiences under water.

Lord Tebbit later wrote in the *Daily Mail*, "We set out with some bags of fish to feed some local turtles, which had given up the work of hunting and now lived on welfare provided by tourists like me." That was a sanitised version of events for public consumption in the national press.

In fact the turtles, expecting food and finding none, simply attacked the man as he tried to fend them off, biting one finger badly in the process. It didn't help that the locals had named the turtle that did the biting, Arthur. Arthur Scargill had been the union leader taken on by Norman Tebbit during an infamous coalminers' strike.

THE AMAZING FROGFISH

Frogfish can consume prey bigger than themselves, but usually they are themselves quite
small.

Strange frogfish exist in most tropical and subtropical seas. They
lead a sedentary life, stumbling around the reef on modified
pectoral fins that function as flabby legs. They are masters of
camouflage and able to mimic precisely the colour of the favourite
sponge they sit on. At first glance they are nothing more than a featureless blob. Unless you know where to look, they usually go unnoticed.
In fact they are so ugly and shapeless, they hardly look like fish at all.

A member of the family Antennariidae, which includes other an-
glerfishes, they lie in wait for the unwary, dangling a lure above their
mouths that has been developed from a modified dorsal spine. It looks
like a little fry or a worm and entices any fish that likes to eat such small
delicacies. It's at this moment that the frogfish strikes.

Frogfish tend to be quite small. Normally, one could sit comfortably
in the palm of a hand. Because they are able to call upon a vast repertoire
of colour schemes, they make popular subjects for divers armed with
extreme close-up cameras, and dive guides around the world tend to
know where they hang out on the reef.

THE AMAZING FROGFISH

Divers seek out frogfish and the waters of East Asia can provide plenty of encounters. The Lembeh Strait in North Suluwesi is famous for the weird and the wonderful, if not macabre marine life, and the frogfish found there come in many different varieties, including the fantastic hairy frogfish. However, there is one place much closer to Europe that can afford a memorable frogfish encounter.

The Gulf of Aqaba is an extension of the African Rift and has deep water close to the shore. It also has some pretty coral reefs that are home to the full gamut of Red Sea marine life. All the usual suspects are there. There are millions of anthiases and glassfish and dozens of lionfish and grouper that prey on them. Eagle rays pass by and electric rays dodge about the sandy patches. Taba is at the Gulf's most northern point, at the border between Egypt and Israel. What makes underwater Taba almost unique though, is its population of giant frogfish.

Frogfish feed on almost anything that moves, but these Taba frogfish are unusual in that they prey on lionfish. Yes, you read that right. These are not the little frogfish in pretty colours more usually encountered elsewhere. These frogfish are big enough to swallow a lionfish!

That's probably why one example often seen, looks so green. Well, you'd feel a bit green if you'd swallowed a fish that's famous for its poisonous spines, wouldn't you? It gives a new perspective to the image of a bulldog that's swallowed a wasp. Frogfish are able to swallow prey fish that are actually bigger than they are. They have rubbery flexible bodies that can encompass almost anything they can suck into their cavernous mouths. The voracious lionfish is tempted to dart in and grab the frogfish's dangled lure. The joke is on the would-be hunter though.

The frogfish is quicker than the unfortunate lionfish. It gulps and in a moment the in-rush of water has dragged the unsuspecting predator-turned-prey into that cavernous interior. It does this in one of the fastest movements of any animal recorded. A frogfish has been scientifically photographed at such a high speed that it's thought to take only around 1/6000 of a second to grab a meal. That's fast food!

Although frogfish are able to change their body colour and texture to mimic their surroundings, these Taba frogfish are quite cocky. They are almost flamboyant in the way they pose magnificently in colours that contrast nicely with their surroundings instead of adopting the colour of the sponge or coral they sit upon.

They walk about on their modified pectoral fins, using them like flexible feet. At around 30 cm (1 ft) long and more, they are easy to spot and if you see one, you're bound to see its partner somewhere nearby, although it's probably wearing a totally different colour scheme. Not only that, although giant frogfish are normally easy to approach, these frogfish actually approach divers.

During one dive at Taba it was reported that a large dark green frogfish, an animal with an appetite bigger than its belly, even came and sat on a diver's head. It must have thought him to be a suitable vantage point and his head a bit of sponge to perch on. When Hugh Watson, the manager of the local diving centre was told of this, he immediately recognised the one described. He recounted how he had been doing an introductory dive and was routinely kneeling on the sand with his trainee, when he spotted the creature bouncing along the featureless, sandy seabed, a long way off from where he was. There was no reef nearby. It bounced purposefully up to him and attached itself to his chest. The trainee diver with him was taken aback, but ever the calm and unflustered Welshman, Hugh was relaxed. It's the sort of thing that happens under water at Taba.

THE AMOROUS
ELEPHANT SEAL

The rule about diving with wild animals is never to interact with them, but rather to let them interact with you – however, things can go horribly wrong.

The Sea of Cortez near Mexico, is a temperate sea with the biggest range of water temperatures of anywhere in the world. At the height of summer, the water can be icy cold or it might be comfortably warm. Who knows?

There is little in the way of coral in the Sea of Cortez, but the ever-changing water temperatures and copious amounts of sunlight combine to produce at times, plankton levels that support massive amounts of marine life. Whale sharks, manta rays and even grey whales are quite common.

That's why Jamie Curtis left the UK, set up a dive centre there and made a new life for himself in this part of Mexico. Jamie was after some much needed publicity for his venture, which is why he soon invited a British diving magazine photographer to visit.

But it's not that easy to find the stars of the show and to dive with them. They are pelagic animals, forever wandering the vast emptiness of the ocean. You need good luck to enjoy an exciting mid-water encounter. So with no coral reefs to speak of, where are the territorial animals that form the reliable and permanent attraction that would make a diver happy to spend valuable vacation time here? Jamie fondly recounts this tale.

Los Islotes are 80 km (50 miles) from the town of La Paz. Some ragged rocks towering from the water, a rough red cake capped with guano like icing-sugar. And what's that noise? Los Islotes is a California sea lion colony or "rookery".

Diving close to California sea lions can be a heart-stopping experience. The females behave like ladies. A graceful, young female quickly investigates what she clearly thinks is a strange air-bubbling creature. She appears in a moment. A pirouette, a brisé, two arabesques and she is gone. There's hardly time to get a successful photograph. The pups behave like naughty children, but the bulls act like angry fathers.

A successful bull will breed with as many females as he can and enthusiastically guards his harem. It has been known for one male to service 40 females. It all depends on his size and strength. Each bull has his own clearly defined territory for which he has fought off other bulls. The males seem to devote most of their time to maintaining a dominant position in that territory. They are large and powerful and will aggressively defend their harem against incursions from other males. That's what all the barking is about.

During the first year that Jamie was set up for diving, an intruder joined the sea lions' rookery. Bigger than any of the massive sea lion males, a solitary young elephant seal had opted to move in with them. He wasn't in any danger from the sea lions but he was obviously very lonely. No doubt they had frequently told him to go off and seek his own kind, but he was looking for love.

The female sea lions may have rejected his amorous advances but he found other more compliant partners in the unsuspecting scuba divers that came to visit the sea lion colony at Los Islotes. The magazine photographer heard about this phenomenon and chose this as his major: it made the perfect photo opportunity.

Photographers can make terrible buddies. The anonymous buddies that chose this photographer to go diving with, probably regret it to this day.

"I would go in with an unsuspecting buddy because I knew exactly what was going to happen," the photographer recalled later. "The elephant seal would position itself above the chosen diver, then wrap its flippers around them. And what do you do if an elephant seal wants to mate with you? Well, there's not a lot you can do."

Naturally, he was partnered with a different unsuspecting buddy each time. There were few that wanted to repeat the experience. Then it nearly went horribly wrong.

As had become usual on each dive, he watched fascinated as the enormous animal stealthily approached its target diver from above and behind, lining him up. However, this time the animal simply swam closely above the other diver, mirroring his movements.

"I was all ready to get this marvellous picture and everything was lined up for the shot. The other guy's swimming along, oblivious to what's happening, and the elephant seal is hovering above him getting ready to grab and do its best. I'm ready with my camera – and then, to my amazement, the elephant seal opens its mouth.

It opened its mouth wider and wider. The animal had teeth reminiscent of piano keys. It then plunged down and encompassed my buddy's head in the voluminous opening.

Instead of taking the all-time, award-winning natural history picture, I resorted to hitting the huge animal as hard as I could with my camera. It was like hitting a sofa with a paper handkerchief. It didn't seem to make much impression, yet it had the desired effect. The elephant seal released his victim, looked at me reproachfully and swam off offended."

Later, at the surface, the other diver asked what happened.

"It suddenly went dark down there."

There are some things that are better left unexplained.

GALAPAGOS WHALE SHARKS

Whale sharks are huge but harmless, and in the Galapagos, a park ranger must accompany you if you want to scuba dive with one.

The Galapagos Islands are volcanic and recently formed. They are by no means to be considered pretty. Most are uninhabited and form a national park, although at the equator 966 km (600 miles) from the coast of Ecuador, the water around these islands is somewhat cold. The archipelago lies at the confluence of two major cold currents from the north and south, which cause a pressure effect that keeps the warmer Pacific water from the west at bay. The climate is therefore equable and quite untropical.

Diving in the Galapagos is a matter of great variety. Nowhere else can you swim alongside tropical species like Moorish idols at the same time as penguins. If you love the rare and unusual, there is the red-lipped batfish or the flightless cormorant. You can snorkel in the shallows with marine iguanas or teams of friendly sea lions. On land, each island, or even each part of an island, offers unusual or endemic terrestrial species, none of which seem to be afraid of man. If your joy is to dive with big pelagic marine life in the Galapagos, I could sum it up in two words: Darwin Island.

This is the most remote and northerly extremity of the archipelago. Darwin himself never made it to the tiny island named after him, but it provides the most spectacular dive site of all. Many divers would be happy to spend a whole dive trip there and nowhere else in the Galapagos.

The solitary dive site is marked by some rocks topped by a natural structure about the same size and shape as the Arc de Triomphe in Paris – Darwin's Arch. The ocean current pushes round in an almost irresistible way and this in turn attracts innumerable big fishes.

You are not allowed to dive here without being accompanied by an official Galapagos naturalist guide or marine park ranger. One such ranger was quick to tell the divers he escorted, that he was known as the "Silver Fox".

During a single dive it is possible to see flotillas of mobulae (small manta-like rays), squadrons of hammerhead sharks out in the middle distance, massed jacks trying to mimic a slow-moving juggernaut, less sociable Galapagos sharks and the occasional lone Risso's dolphin that continuously dives around where divers cling on to the rocky substrate, in the strongly flowing current, watching the show.

Most spectacular of all are the whale sharks. Whale sharks are the biggest fish in the ocean and are so named because they feed in the same way as the great baleen whales. These ocean-roving juggernauts follow the plankton on which they feed, huge mouths agape, insatiably filtering the water for the tiniest forms of life. They are also known to vacuum up great schools of small fish by approaching them from below, mouths open wide, so that they are scooped up helplessly en masse. They represent no danger to larger animals including man.

Whale sharks can be encountered almost anywhere in the tropical or subtropical zone, but by the time they have reached the lonely outpost of Darwin Island in the Pacific, they have reached maturity and their full size. They can measure up to 18 m (59 ft) long. Can you imagine what it is like to meet an animal with the dimensions of a big intercontinental truck swimming majestically through the water with unhurried sweeps of its massive tail? Can you imagine what it must be like to come face

21

to face with a group of them? At Darwin's Arch they are often seen in groups.

Unhurried they may look, but these spotty monsters meander at about 2 knots, which is as fast as a fully-equipped scuba diver can sustain for a short period. Divers leave the safety of the reef wall and take their chances with the current in exchange for a few moments with the whale sharks in the blue water. It's undeniable that it's a special experience to swim alongside a fish that makes a man feel like a minnow. One can only keep up for a limited amount of time before they sweep on past, but luckily these animals circumnavigate Darwin Island several times, allowing the superb experience to be repeated again and again.

It's tempting for any diver to try to grab hold of a passing dorsal fin and hitch a ride on one of these giant yet benign creatures, but any modern and enlightened environmentalist would frown at the practice. It was, however, an impulse that the Silver Fox could not suppress. He grabbed a dorsal fin of a passing whale shark and rode the animal, Calgary Stampede style, for about three minutes as it circled in confusion round the incredulous audience.

That was not enough. Whale sharks are not the most intelligent organisms on the planet and are in fact, very docile. The Silver Fox went on to do something that anyone who was not there to witness it, would not have believed. He dragged himself forwards along the top of the animal's head and tumbled headfirst into its openly gaping maw. For a moment he disappeared Jonah-like, until with a great rush of water and the diver's own accumulated exhaled bubbles he was expelled in slight disarray, while the creature, with a gentle sweep of its mighty tail, turned and unhurriedly swam on its way.

LIBERTY IN BALI

A diver takes a liberty in Bali when he drags a reluctant buddy from his sleep to accompany him.

S iddhartha was the first Buddha and Barbara, the dive centre manager, was god. She explained to the visiting diver that solo diving was not allowed at the new Siddhartha dive resort on Bali's northern coast.

That's why he had to persuade Robert, the Austrian dive guide and Barbara's monitor, to get up before first light to come with him. As it was, Robert was rather slow getting into his kit because he was still wiping the sleep from his eyes, while the keen visitor was already striding, rigged to dive and camera in hand, down from the empty car park to Tulamben's stony beach and the water's edge.

Normally, there are bands of tiny lady porters who only weigh around 35 kg (80 lb) and have legs like sticks, defying logic as they carry up to three fully rigged tanks on their heads. They sprint down across the slippery stones in their flipflops, while their hefty first-world clients stumble along behind. These ladies didn't start work before daybreak, so it was do-it-yourself for him this time. No problem.

Adrenaline helps achieve things normally found difficult, and he was a little angry. Their driver had turned up an hour late, and already the tropical sun was twinkling over the horizon.

He never faltered as he strode out through the shallows, coping with breaking waves. The seabed was heavily strewn with highly polished stones, some of them the size of bowling balls.

The previous afternoon he had stumbled and cursed, as he struggled out into water deep enough to swim in. Today was different – but why, you may be wondering, was he so keen to get into the water?

Just off the beach lie the mangled remains of an armed World War II freighter, built in 1918 and damaged by a Japanese torpedo during the Pacific conflict. Two American destroyers towed the crippled vessel to the shore at Tulamben, where it was beached, unloaded and then abandoned in the face of the Japanese advance. There it stayed in shallow water, used by locals as a good place from which to fish.

It lay there for years, part of the scenery and rusting away until 1963, when Bali's most active volcano, Mount Agung, exploded. Indonesia's President Sukarno had invited seismologists and volcanologists from all over the world to witness the expected eruption, but they got the date wrong.

The remains of the USS *Liberty* were finally trashed forever and rolled into the sea, along with tons of stones and lava – and a thousand people who had tragically returned to their homes at the water's edge, in the mistaken belief that it was all a false alarm.

Lying at between 10 m (33 ft) and 30 m (100 ft) deep, and hardly now recognisable as a wreck, USS *Liberty* had become Bali's favourite reef, albeit an artificial one. Its twisted and torn remains had become home to countless animals, from giant barracuda to the tiniest pygmy seahorse.

The stern of the wreck was still recognizable, but its two guns, one fallen with its turret to the black volcanic sand, were so profusely covered in corals and sponges that you needed a detailed briefing to understand what they were.

Bali's waters are so fertile with life that divers are discouraged from clearing their masks with their eyes open. Something might be encouraged to hatch out in your sinuses!

The hold area of the wreck is full of silver jacks, hiding presumably, from the barracuda. A few spars here reveal this reef's history as a ship, but apart from the old wheel, most of the steel is smothered in growth, including gorgonia and large barrel sponges.

The *Liberty* is a prime example of Mother Nature reclaiming her territory.

Striped Sergeant Majors guard their great tracts of eggs, laid on algae-clad steel plates, against marauders. Glassfish cluster in shady alcoves and during daylight hours, schooling divers are regularly silhouetted against the brightly lit surface; while open-water students practise their skills in the shallows, kneeling on the black volcanic sand.

As Bali's most famous dive site, the *Liberty* gets as busy with divers as it does with marine life. But this still doesn't explain the anxiety to get into the water and into the wreckage just before dawn.

A couple of weeks earlier, the visiting diver had been at Sha'ab Rumi in Sudan, where he had struggled to get good close-ups of the herds of bumphead parrotfish that graze the coral reefs. He called them herds because these fish look like marine bison, as they crunch their way across the reef.

That said, they are good bluffers – sideways on they have a massive build, but when they turn towards you they look like cardboard cut-outs.

He had heard that the wreckage of the *Liberty* was used by a vast school of bumphead parrotfish as a safe place to roost at night. He wanted to get the shots before they left at dawn.

Alas, the tardiness of their driver meant that he met them streaming out from their overnight quarters just as he arrived on-site, but luckily, just like Robert, they were still wiping the sleep from their eyes.

He guessed they weren't expecting to meet a diver so early in the morning, and they seemed quite bemused to see him. Admittedly, the daylight gave him a pleasant blue background to his shots, but he had to work quickly. There were still stragglers in the wreck and these were the ones he needed to locate, and fast.

Every moment that passed equated to a moment of diminished opportunity. The sluggishness exhibited by these odd-looking characters was quickly passing and some of them dashed back into the wreck for cover, ironically going exactly where he wanted them to be.

He felt a bit like a police bust-team, catching the suspects in their beds and gathering the evidence in a blast of light. Wow! He thought he had captured some nice pictures before they were all gone, escaping into the open ocean for the day.

Still dripping with seawater, he strolled back out of the water, passing the first of the Balinese porters carrying the gear of early risers down to the shore.

Robert was waiting for him in the car park, where he took a refreshing shower and rinsed his kit. He didn't remember seeing him in the water, but he must have been there. They don't allow solo diving at Siddhartha.

THIS DUGONG
DON'T CARE!

The dugong is a strange marine mammal and
may make a rare encounter for a diver, unless
you know where to go.

R ami had come from San Diego, California, and was tracing his
Egyptian roots. He now lived close to Marsa Alam. He often
dived along this coast. He knew that a dugong frequented a
certain bay. Other divers had seen it but he had only encountered huge
green turtles and a few guitar sharks on previous visits, when he was
diving from a boat. Now there was a recently constructed hotel on the
beach and he and his buddy were land-based.

They were prepared to spend all week if necessary, searching for the
elusive dugong, but there was no need. It might have been a remote
bay on Egypt's Red Sea coast, but the presence of the new hotel resort
meant things were different. They had been told that they only had to
sit on the now crowded holiday beach in their dive kit, and wait until
they saw 20 or 30 Italian holidaymakers becoming hysterical, yelling
and screaming and splashing above the dugong, to know where it was.
Sure enough, before long a shout went up from one man and all the

other people in the water began to swim hastily, if not too neatly to where it was.

The divers leapt into action, grabbing their underwater cameras and wading out in the shallows until it was deep enough to swim. When they had got out there, they could not believe what they saw. The dugong was in only about 3 m (10 ft) of water and within easy reach of those prepared to hold their breath and swim down. Above it was an uncontrolled mob, splashing and kicking, with dozens of flipper-clad feet bicycling frantically.

The animal seemed totally unperturbed, lumbering along on its foreleg-like flippers, grazing on the grass cow-like with its capacious, bristly snout. It occasionally rose quietly in an almost stately manner through the melee to take a breath of air, before returning serenely to the bottom to continue feeding.

It was the scuba divers that were perturbed. Swimming below the holidaymakers, their cameras were kicked by endless numbers of feet. Their breathing regulators were continually wrenched from their mouths by the wayward limbs of swimmers that hurtled down and crashed into them. They got bruises in places they didn't know they had. They were having a tough time and wondered why the creature stayed in such shallow water, but the dugong didn't seem to give a damn. It did have numerous old scars on its back, but before you think that nails or jewellery carelessly caused these injuries, be informed that male dugongs have tusks that they use in a cavalier manner during the mating season. Not only that, this animal appeared to be quite a clumsy swimmer when it came to manoeuvring. It was a bit cow-like. It's said that when the wind gets up and waves form in the bay, it had sometimes been seen crashing carelessly against the nearby coral reef. Clumsy cow!

It wasn't a pretty animal either. About the size of a cow and reminiscent of a little underwater elephant from the front, the dugong is a large marine mammal that has a wide tail with a fluke not unlike that of a whale. It gives rise to the idea that when sailors from Europe first encountered them and glimpsed them from a distance, carrying their offspring in an arm-like posture of the forward flipper, the sailors may have originated the legend of the half-human half-fish, the "mermaid".

Dugongs stay under water for only short periods because unlike other marine mammals, they can't hold their breath for very long. This is probably another reason why they like shallow water. Many people confuse dugongs with the freshwater manatees of Florida. In fact they look quite different, especially considering that incongruous tail. In fact the dugong looks quite absurd. Who in their right mind would have designed an aquatic elephant with the tail of a whale and the eating habits of a cow?

Now if you were to leave a cow to graze in a field there would be plenty of evidence of its passing. You'd have to take care where you walked. There was none of that on the seagrass-covered seabed thanks to the voracious activities of the huge and obviously well-fed remoras that travelled with the dugong, quietly getting on with the job of cleaning up as they went – a work in progress.

In fact, life seemed to be carrying on as normal for the dugong. If it didn't like the madding crowd it would have gone somewhere else. Rami and his buddy were only relieved when its path of lush seagrass led it down to 9 m (30 ft) deep, a place where the raucous revellers above, were less able to reach and interfere with them. They could then swim around it without being distracted by the sudden rushes from above and unfortunate impacts by unskilled swimmers, and get the photographs of the dugong in a more natural state. At one point Rami lay on the grass ahead of the animal to get a low-angle photograph as it lumbered over him, as if he wasn't there. It was only afterwards that he realised the pictures of this unusual animal with the madding crowd, told more of a story. This dugong evidently didn't care. Give it plenty of seagrass, and don't bother it.

FISH 'N' CHIPS AT RIBBON REEF NO. 10

A world famous dive site with some spectacular residents, and it's not just the potato cod.

The only way to fully appreciate the vast size of the Great Barrier Reef is to see it from a plane. It is not a single reef but a system of reefs that extend down Australia's east coast from close by Papua New Guinea to the Tropic of Capricorn. It's around 2414 km (1500 miles) long and is made up of over two-and-a-half thousand individual reefs. Some of them have inauspicious names like Ribbon Reef No. 10.

It was probably famous filmmakers and shark experts Ron and Valerie Taylor, that first discovered the giant groupers that lived at Ribbon Reef No. 10, near Lizard Island. It is well documented that while filming with them at that location in the early days, iconic film cameraman Stan Waterman surfaced in great excitement and said, "We've got the fish. All we need now are the potatoes!"

Ever the anglophile and a well-read gentleman to boot, but as an American not quite getting the original English vernacular quite right, Stan was referring to the main components of English "fish and chips", or even more accurately, cod and chips. Chips in England are known elsewhere as French fries. Never mind the colloquial inaccuracy, the name stuck and the giant groupers forever after, were known as the potato cod and the place is now known as the Cod Hole.

Martha Holmes and Mike deGruy presented a segment of the revolutionary 1991 BBC documentary, *Sea Trek* at the Cod Hole. It was revolutionary because they wore bubble helmets and for the first time, could address the audience both visibly and orally while under water, but all that viewers seem to remember of what Martha said to camera was, "It's quite extraordinary!"

In her book of the series, she reported that the largest hermaphrodite fish they came across were the most common reef-dwelling predators, the groupers. The most impressive were at the world-famous Cod Hole.

Martha described the fish as being coloured light grey with darker blotches and that they were simply huge, weighing around 100 kg (220 lb) each. She told that within a minute, they were surrounded. Occasionally these giants would rush at each other, demonstrating that they had some sort of hierarchy that had been violated and reminding those watching of their extraordinary power. She deduced they also had a curious nature and seemed to solicit strokes as well as enjoy being tickled under the chin. Martha didn't mention the feeding.

A more comprehensive account of the diving was made by a writer from Britain's *Diver* magazine.

"We finally arrived at Ribbon Reef No. 10 and the Cod Hole, the focus of the trip aboard our giant catamaran *Spoilsport*. Here numerous large potato cod and sometimes one Maori wrasse had grown accustomed to being hand-fed.

The feeder wears a chain-mail glove, because big grouper have sharp teeth. Some of the guest divers were clearly alarmed at being so close to such large animals. You can get as close as you like to the action. I photographed the feed, and then got some rewarding shots of a potato cod under the boat.

The last dive was to be at the same location. Craig, the dive manager aboard our vessel, asked what I thought of the trip. Now, I confess to being utterly spoiled. I appreciated that everyone was enjoying the trip but suggested that it was all rather tame. One could never see the best of what was there by always diving in the shadow of a boat the size of an office block, in the lee of any current, and in the company of a shoal of flapping divers.

Craig confirmed that most of the divers were very inexperienced and that the safety of the operation was paramount. Then he offered to let me dive alone, on the opposite side of the reef to the Cod Hole, at the current point. It was where the irresistible ocean flow of the Coral Sea met the immovable object of the reef. He warned me that there would be a fearsome current and took me out in the inflatable, the emergency diver's pick-up boat.

The current proved to be exhilarating rather than fearsome. I tucked in close to the reef so that there would be no danger of being sent off into the open sea, and drifted along past some of the finest table corals I had ever seen. They had built up on the reef in layers, so looked more like plate corals at first glance. Coral growth flourishes when fed by a steady flow of oxygenated water.

A great shadow passed over me. Was it a whale shark? No, it was a school of densely packed bumphead parrotfish. These strange looking animals feed by eating live coral, biting it off the reef with their strong beaks. It is said that most of the white sand encountered on tropical beaches has passed through the gut of animals like this at some time. They dumped a load of processed coral sand over me as they continued onwards and disappeared over the reef top.

There were plenty more potato cod to look at, though these spotty giants looked puny compared to three massively built blue-black Queensland grouper that came within chin-tickling distance and gave me lots of portrait shots. Plenty of white-tip reef sharks were enjoying the flow too and then I found myself confronted by one of the biggest sharks I had ever seen.

It was facing me, lying mortally injured on the sandy bottom, but hard to recognise. Its head had been smashed in – its eyes were gone. Its wound was covered in small fish that were feeding on it. Green blood pulsed into the water, half a dozen remoras dashed around in panic. What could have caused such a horrific injury?

I fired off one picture. The shark sensed my presence and turned away, crashing into the reef. Its head must have been a metre across. I saw its two dorsal fins – it was the biggest tawny nurse shark I had ever seen and it was dying, but there was no way I could follow it against the flow.

The vessel I was on was equipped with prop guards, and it was unlikely such a bottom-feeder would be swimming close enough to the surface to be hit by a boat.

Another vessel had been seen with fishermen aboard near the reef when we arrived. I believe they had hooked this animal and, unable to land it in the boat alive, tried to kill it by smashing its head in while it was still in the water. It had escaped the hook during the violence. What a shameful thing."

MANTA IN THE MIST

Left alone with a feeding giant manta may be any diver's dream but it might be a nightmare if things aren't planned properly.

Bobbing around with his head just above the surface of a calm sea, there was only the sound of the water rippling about Rob's neck, and the occasional "flip, flap" of the giant Pacific manta's wing tips as and when they broke the surface. The animal, around 7 m (23 ft) across, circled round while he waited patiently with his camera.

He thought of Hemingway's *Old Man and the Sea*. In that novel the old man battled to land a giant fish in a cockleshell of a craft. Rob, on the other hand, was equipped with little more than a pair of fins, a mask and snorkel. He wore a skimpy pair of shorts that left him wincing from the stings of a billion zooplankton and it was the same plankton the manta was enjoying feeding on.

The boat had dropped them off about 3.5 km (2 miles) from shore, but Rob's wife found the plankton just too painful to endure. She had retreated to the boat, but he had asked the crew to move the boat away and leave him there.

The boat was now so far off he couldn't pick it out against the backdrop in the faltering evening light. So it was just man and the manta.

Flip, flap. Its small dorsal fin gave away its position, along with the two enormous white remoras that rode in parallel position on its back, heads out of the water. They looked for all the world like a pair of matching gargoyles. How did they manage to breathe, let alone survive the scorching Mexican sun?

The whole scene was more gothic than any creation on celluloid. No wonder these mantas are often called devilfish.

Each time the manta and its entourage appeared to turn his way, Rob slipped vertically beneath the surface, exhaling through his snorkel so that he would drop without a telltale splash. The water was like warm vichyssoise, thick with rich nutrients and stinging nematocysts.

Unless he positioned himself on a collision course with the manta, he had no chance of seeing it under water. The visibility was a thick mist. The few times he got lucky he squeezed off a frame of film and received a swipe from a wing tip in reprimand for his success. Close encounters of this kind were infrequent, and he was rewarded with a dozen frames shot with a close focusing, super-wide-angle lens over the course of more than an hour.

The water was comfortable at 30°C (86°F) and Rob was buoyant enough to keep his head well clear of the surface while floating upright, but he began to rue his enthusiasm to be left alone in such a vast expanse of water. He wondered just how many stings he could take as he anxiously scanned the surface for a possible encounter with a highly poisonous Portuguese man-of-war. Meanwhile, the manta was circling further from him.

Then, just as it appeared to be all over, the ocean around him began to boil with a glittering mass of thousands of small fish, beating the surface in synchronised panic. It was as if the cloudless heavens had opened with a tropical deluge, but this was no rain. His heart paused for a moment, full with the dread of the unknown. He was relieved to see the dorsal and sweeping tailfin of a whaleshark as it casually rounded up its dinner. Strangely, he felt equally relieved when this meandering behemoth of the ocean went on its way. It had spooked him. The dense cloud of plankton was obviously attracting everything that fed on it.

Only an hour or so earlier, he'd just finishing packing to go home. Rob lay dozing on the big hotel bed. It had been an eventful and exhausting week. The phone rang. "Six giant Pacific mantas and a whaleshark in the bay!"

When you want encounters with pelagic animals, you have to be prepared to drop everything. That's the name of the game in the Gulf of California, also known as the Sea of Cortez. Getting the telephone message, he ran down to the dock, accompanied by his wife, with underwater camera, masks, fins and snorkel in hand, to where the dive centre's boat waited.

Now he needed to wait. The boat had almost disappeared towards the coast. The sun was threatening to disappear below the horizon. He realised that he too was disappearing from sight.

Flip, flap. The manta returned. It was feeding on the plankton, doing what it always did. Circling around, making barrel rolls, huge mouth agape, enjoying the now cooling air of a Mexican evening. The plankton chased the fading daylight, getting ever closer to the surface. The manta, nature's marine vacuum cleaner, hoovered up the feast. It was getting darker.

When Rob, in his faltering Spanish, had asked the boatman to take the boat away, he hadn't considered the possibility of a misunderstanding that he would take it away altogether. He'd meant just to heave to at a sufficient distance not to disturb the feeding giant.

Luckily, his wife was on the boat. She spoke no Spanish at all but he was sure that she would see the problem and they'd come back before it was too late. If he'd planned properly to do this he would have at least armed himself with a signal lamp.

Flip, flap. The manta got on with the business in hand just as it always had and always would, circling round, those two giant remoras breaking the surface now like matching ornate figureheads. Rob was beginning to feel very lonely.

It was a great experience but sometimes these things need to be shared, especially with someone in a boat.

Without warning, the manta breached for a moment. It made a great splash and was gone. Rob felt abandoned by both animal and man. He started to get really frightened until he heard a friendly shout from his wife in the last rays of the setting sun. He was relieved to be saved and simultaneously ecstatic.

WHY DOLPHINS SMILE

Dolphins have always had a special relationship with man, perhaps because they like to come up and take a cheeky look into our world – or is it because of that permanent smile?

Why do they smile? The biological answer is that a dolphin is a mammal and as such, needs fresh water which it gets from the fish it eats, by swallowing them whole, using its teeth merely for gripping. Inevitably, it takes in a gulp of seawater with its lunging bite, so the rear of the mouth is used to eject the seawater squashed up by its tongue. They are messy eaters and many of their prey escape injured.

It is important to note that swimming with dolphins in blue water has its risks. Jeremy Stafford-Deitsch won't forget the time he dropped in with a huge pod, only to discover an equally huge school of at least 100 grey reef, silky and silver-tip sharks below them, ready to clear up the mess of wounded fish that had escaped the dolphins.

Splashing about at the surface, involuntarily doing an impression of a sick or wounded mammal, will invite a speedy response from these predators, and possibly an investigative bite. The sharks rushed up to meet Jeremy. He does not recommend the experience.

There have been stories about people being rescued from shark attacks by dolphins, but perhaps if they had not been swimming with the dolphins, they might not have attracted the attention of the accompanying sharks.

Perhaps we have an affinity with dolphins because they breathe air like us and spend a lot of time swimming near the surface. Alone among sea-dwellers, it is whales and dolphins which reveal their presence when they breathe.

Because of this, they were a great deal less mysterious to ancient peoples than other creatures of the deep, and healing powers were attributed to them.

Stories of dolphins rescuing drowning people predate Flipper by many centuries and there have been many accounts of dolphins preferring the company of humans to that of their own kind.

JoJo is a male dolphin that became an icon for Provo in the Turks & Caicos Islands – that is, until he started becoming too amorous with the occasional long-haired female diver. As one witness stated, "Goodness, I've never seen anything like it!" JoJo is an oddball, a social outcast dolphin that sought friendship with man instead of his own kind, and one man in particular, Dean Bernal. JoJo is one of the few truly wild dolphins to have been subject to study.

There are other examples. A female spotted dolphin once buddied up with a young deaf-mute Bedouin man at the village of Mezzina in the Egyptian Sinai, south of Nuweiba. Abdullah and his family turned their friendship into a useful additional source of income when they got people to pay to either scuba or snorkel with the unlikely partnership.

This dolphin, Oline, mated with passing wild males, but sadly none of her offspring survived for long. She preferred the company of her human friend. This friend provided a brick with which divers could stroke the animal, such is the toughness of a dolphin's hide.

In Sanctuary Bay on Grand Bahama there is a centre that tries to rehabilitate any bottlenose dolphin rescued from dolphinaria and aquaria. The large and impressive animals are free to leave at any time but prefer to stay since they are fed with Canadian herring every day. They even breed and now their offspring live with them in extended family groups.

Divers can pay to swim with the dolphins and are usually accompanied by a couple of animals. It's a very rewarding experience. The dolphins know what is expected of them and have a repertoire of poses and acts for the benefit of underwater cameras. After an hour, they know uncannily that it's time to swim back to their low-sided pens.

More than 40 000 visitors a year visit Monkey Mia at Sharks Bay in Western Australia, where wild bottlenose dolphins have made it a habit to voluntarily strand themselves to meet people!

Monkey Mia is assumed to be named after HMS *Monkey* and the aborigine word moa, or "home". Its dolphins are the only wild herd in the world to have befriended humans in this way. First noticed back in 1964, they have become a big tourist attraction, but the dolphins seem unconcerned for the moment.

Around Britain and Ireland, the same phenomenon of the lone dolphin has occurred. After seeing his young son lifted out of the water by a dolphin known as Donald in the Isle of Man in 1974, Dr Horace Dobbs gave up his career as a research scientist to swim and scuba with dolphins, to study them, write books and lecture on the subject.

He attributes healing and therapeutic properties to dolphins and reckons that clinically depressed people who get the opportunity to enjoy a close encounter with them benefit from the experience. Donald went on to become a well-known character in the waters off Ireland, Wales and Cornwall.

Another solitary dolphin, which lived off Godrevy Island near St Ives between 1981 and 1984, was Percy. He became something of a celebrity and a tourist attraction, though fame eventually went to his head, and he became aggressive and started exhibiting indiscriminate sexual behaviour. He was reported as attacking a windsurfer, and caused rifts among the locals, who had different ideas about how to treat him.

The following winter, Percy vanished. But Fungie, another man-friendly dolphin, frequented Dingle Bay in southwest Ireland, and a Risso's dolphin, a stout-bodied species without a pronounced beak, was regularly sighted off the Welsh coast.

What is obvious is that these solitary dolphins are in no way normal. Most are male, and their affinity to man might be considered an aberration that is not necessarily entirely healthy.

Like captive dolphins, these individuals can become sexually precocious. One hapless diver was involved in a legal action when he was witnessed by a boatload of dolphin-watchers apparently doing something indecent with Freddie, a friendly dolphin that frequented the area near Amble, in Northumberland.

Horace Dobbs later testified in court that it was more likely the male dolphin trying to do something indecent to the diver, and a "not guilty" verdict was recorded.

Dolphins have a very large, fibrous penis, nearly 2 m (6 ft) long once excited, which is held within the sheath or prepuce inside the body until it becomes erect. Is that another reason for that enigmatic smile? As Dr Dobbs said later, "I thought everyone knew. All these male dolphins do that!" Embarrassed by the incident, Freddie has since decided to relocate.

PART TWO

Interesting Characters and Difficult Moments

LIFE IN THE FAST LANE

The lagoon at Aldabra is the size of Manhattan Island and it fills and empties with each tide through three narrow channels that provide the scuba ride of your life.

Twice a day, the water empties out of the Aldabra lagoon with the falling tide into the Indian Ocean and then refills with the incoming tide. It also washes out all the fishes that browse for their food within it. As the tide turns, the fishes congregate at the mouths of the three channels that feed the lagoon. They wait to get back in. There is Main channel, East channel and Johnny channel.

The inflatable boat drops divers in the ocean outside Main channel. A couple of female passengers from the diving liveaboard *Indian Ocean Explorer*, wish to do it by snorkelling at the surface. The sea has a huge swell and it's good to exchange the discomfort of a bouncing dinghy for the weightlessness of the deep. Thousands of fishes hover in silent aggregation but their relaxed appearance belies a current that is already moving at more than one knot.

The divers cling to the rocks. They are envious of the one with the reef hook that allows him a hands-free approach. Another diver hangs on to him. He is impressed that his hook and buoyancy control is strong enough for both of them. Then they decide they have waited long enough and let themselves go with the flow.

Main channel is about 30 m (100 ft) deep in the middle. It is several hundred metres wide. The underwater visibility drops to around 10 m (32 ft) and one diver soon loses sight of the others. He bowls along with the landscape rolling below him. He finds it hard to maintain one depth. He tries to keep at 22 m (70 ft) but one moment he is deeper and the next he is racing near to the surface. The currents have an up and down aspect to them too it seems.

Giant groupers and huge potato cod rush out from hiding to inspect him as he passes. They are waiting in ambush for smaller prey than he. Massive bumphead parrotfish veer away out of sight. Every rocky arch he passes seems to be hiding some underwater warrior ready to gobble up the unwary. It's like a giant computer game and he is in it.

Forty minutes pass. Our solo diver begins to wonder where the others are. He works out that the closer to the stationary underwater surfaces of the island you travel, the slower you go. He heads out into deeper water to put on a bit of speed for five minutes and then heads back.

Miracle upon miracle, he joins the main group. "Where have you just come from?" is written all over their faces. They can't wait for the next rising tide to do it all again.

They wait until next day before they go in again with the inward flow. It would be rather silly to do it with the outward flow. Who knows where you would end up? The solo diver heads off on his own again. This time he goes for the left-hand side of the channel. Everyone else seems to opt for the right. It's another fast ride a bit like a *Star Wars* X-wing ride. When he surfaces he has left the turbulent water of the ocean behind and is in a tranquil, flat, turquoise sea. About half a mile in one direction he makes out a small cluster of figures around a safety sausage. He can see another safety sausage a mile behind him. He erects his surface marker flag.

But there is no diver pick-up boat in sight. Only the *Indian Ocean Explorer* is visible at anchor in the ocean beyond the channel, and still coasting on a fast current, he soon loses sight of that behind the low coral islands that rise above the walls of the lagoon.

Remembering that the water flows more quickly where it is deep, he uses his flag as a sail to send him out into the middle. The furthest group appear to be swimming towards him but they are not. They, like him, are still travelling into the lagoon but he is travelling faster. He uses his flag to vector his course back to them. They are amazed at his newly found sailing skills. Quite frankly, so is he.

David Rowat, the captain of *Indian Ocean Explorer*, is in this group. He's suffering a sense of humour failure. Where is the pick-up boat? They are in the confines of a lagoon. It may be as big as Manhattan but there are no tall buildings to become obscured by. They know it is just a question of waiting. The only hazard seems to be getting torn on fire coral as they rattle past it.

Eventually the inflatable pick-up boat arrives. They have been waiting 30 minutes. The snorkellers had blown the plan and decided to stay outside the channel in the ocean. The boat crew had wisely opted to stay with them and pick them up first. One reports that the yellow surface-marker flag is far more visible than the orange safety sausages. Rowat makes a mental note to order a number for the boat so that all the future passengers can have them.

Next day they decide to up the voltage somewhat. They dive East channel. It is much narrower. At 22 m (65 ft) to the bottom you can still see both sides. It's a narrow gorge. The water is moving like a torrent.

Two divers hurtle along together, following the bottom. Another guest diver and the captain are just ahead. There are shifting banks of sand that act like speed bumps. You never know what's on the other side. They make a mental note to avoid impacting with stingrays that might be browsing there. No rays are evident, but in quick succession they each have a close encounter with a large nurse shark. A giant grouper hurtles out and checks his make-up in the reflective glass dome port of an underwater camera, before ducking back under the cover of a rock. Ahead they see Rowat, dragged by his surface marker buoy on its line, lift his legs to let a bull shark hurtle under. Everyone goes up. They are doing around ten knots and the bull shark is doing at least the same against the flow. That's a closing speed of 20 knots. The photos taken are not perfectly sharp but then what would you expect?

Seventeen minutes into the dive they are back in shallow water. They surface and see the pick-up boat waiting. It's a rush to get every bit of kit into it as they pass. The boat has a strong wind behind, opposing the flow of the water. The divers climb in ecstatic. Captain Rowat tells them that there were in fact two bull sharks, coupled in love until he almost crashed into them. One came out and the other went into the lagoon, both in panic.

"Let's do it again," suggests one diver.

This time cameras are left behind in the boat. The current is even faster. They belt through the channel, passing another nurse shark, but it seems they've already startled the major part of the wildlife. It's all over in only 11 minutes.

The boat is right there. Getting back in the boat is done more slickly this time. They know what to expect and take their aqualung sets off before they get there. It's up and over the inflatable tubes while the crew pull in their tanks. "You came too quickly!" exclaims one overexcited woman diver to the boatman.

Then there is Johnny channel. This is the really fast one – probably 15 knots. They motor slowly through it against the flow in the inflatable. It twists and turns among the mangroves. No one is rushed to get in the water. It's not for the faint-hearted. If you like to dive with pretty fish in swimming pool conditions, don't bother to apply!

THE MYSTERY OF
COMMANDER CRABB

The story of a famous and heroic wartime diver who disappeared after the war in what seemed like very mysterious circumstances.

Lionel Crabb, a pioneering Royal Navy frogman, received the George Cross in 1944 for his work removing Italian limpet mines from Allied merchant ships in Gibraltar Harbour. He remained in the Navy after the war, rising to the rank of commander, and was later said to have helped to inspire Ian Fleming's fictional British spy James Bond. His activities certainly inspired the 1958 British movie, *The Silent Enemy*, starring Laurence Harvey in the part of Crabb.

After the war Crabb continued to dive as a civilian. He explored the wreck of a Spanish galleon and investigated a suitable discharge site for a pipe from the atomic weapons station at Aldermaston. He later returned to the Royal Navy and after helping rescue men trapped in a submarine, he was promoted to the rank of commander. He retired at the age of 55.

It is claimed that in March 1956, Crabb received an urgent message to meet privately with Lord Mountbatten, the First Sea Lord. Crabb was told that he was needed for a secret mission and that the results were to be shared with MI6 and the CIA. During the next few weeks, a CIA agent, Matthew Smith, spent a considerable time with Crabb. The mission involved spying on the Russian cruiser *Ordkhonikidze*, the ship that was going to bring Nikita Khrushchev and Nikolai Bulganin on a goodwill mission to Britain. There were details of the hull that the intelligence agencies were keen to know about. Some say Mountbatten warned Crabb that it was a dangerous mission. The Soviets had discovered earlier that there had been secret dives around the *Sverdlov* when that Russian cruiser visited England in 1955.

On 19th April 1956 Crabb dived into Portsmouth Harbour where the *Ordkhonikidze* was moored. He did not return and it was assumed that he had been either captured or killed by the Russians. With the help of the intelligence services, the Admiralty attempted to cover up the attempt to spy on the Russian ship. On 29th April the Admiralty announced that Crabb had gone missing after taking part in trials of underwater apparatus in Stokes Bay, 5 km (3 miles) from Portsmouth.

When later a body was found in Pagham Harbour and lifted from the water, the head fell off and disappeared. The hands were already gone. Only the old-fashioned, Navy frogman drysuit permitted some sort of identification. The authorities stated it was the last remains of the missing frogman.

However, the story of Commander Crabb wasn't allowed to die for the next 40 years because nobody believed that he was really dead. The popular press turned his disappearance into an everlasting mystery story. Some thought he had been captured or defected and was living a life of luxury in Moscow.

It was one of the most enduring mysteries of the Cold War and if he were dead, who killed him?

Later, Eduard Koltsov, a retired Russian frogman, claimed that he had cut the British diver's throat in Portsmouth Harbour when he caught him placing a mine on the hull of the ship that had brought Nikita Khrushchev and other Soviet leaders to Britain.

According to a BBC News report at that time, Koltsov spoke to a Russian documentary team because he needed to tell the truth before his own death, but the claim was dismissed. It was unthinkable that the

British government or anyone working for it, would have deliberately endangered a visiting ship and all those on it in an English harbour.

Mr Koltsov was 23 at the time of the ship's visit and said that he was ordered to investigate suspicious activity around the ship when he spotted a diver fixing a mine to the hull. He showed the documentary team the dagger he claimed to use to kill the Englishman, and the Red Star medal that he was later secretly awarded for his bravery.

"I saw a silhouette of a diver in a light frogman suit who was fiddling with something at the starboard side, next to the ship's ammunition stores," Mr Koltsov told the film crew, according to the BBC. "I swam closer and saw that he was fixing a mine."

Journalist Yigal Serna later made this story less credible because of an investigation he made in Israel. He had heard that an immigrant to his country in 1990 claimed he knew how Crabb had died. The man was Joseph Zverkin, a former head of Soviet Naval Intelligence. He had spent some time undercover as a spy in England during the 1950s.

Serna was fascinated by the Crabb mystery. He arranged a meeting with Zverkin, who was suspicious about questions regarding Crabb, and refused at first to discuss the matter. Later in a report sent to Britain's *Diver* magazine by Nic Flemming, Yigal Serna reveals what Zverkin finally told him.

"Only at our third meeting did he tell me about Crabb," writes Flemming of Serna's interview with Zverkin. "He spoke in very precise, heavily accented English. He said that in 1956, when the event happened, he was in England, under the code name of a German citizen."

Zverkin's own words recount what happened.

"Crabb was discovered by a watchman when he was seen swimming on the surface of the water next to the ship. An order was given to inspect the water and two people on the deck were equipped with sniper guns – small calibre. One of them was an ordinary seaman, and the other an officer, the equivalent of a lieutenant, who was in charge of an artillery unit on the boat, and an exceptionally good shot.

Crabb must have dived next to the boat and came up and swum on the surface. The lieutenant shot him in the head and killed him. He sank. All the stories about him being caught by us or that he was a Russian spy are not true."

So it seems that the famous World War II diver Commander Crabb, out of luck or out of practice with a pure oxygen rebreather used for covert operations, either suffered oxygen poisoning, a flood of his CCR unit or simply lost control of his buoyancy or even his orientation, broke the surface and was shot. He may have even raced for the surface, mortally injured after the Russian frogman's knife attack. If it's true it makes an unromantic end to a long-running mystery.

THE BLACK HOLE
OF ANDROS

Who would want to dive in a prehistoric chemical cocktail? It seems there are a few candidates!

"I remember the milkiness of the water, and that at 18 m (60 ft) we had been stopped by what looked like a weird mud floor, even though I was sure I had measured around 47 m (152 ft) from the surface earlier. I touched the floor and received the shock of my life. There was no floor – nothing but warmth.

I pulled my hand back so fast that my buddy took a tumble in the water. I had never experienced anything like it. I then buried my hand up to my elbow, then a leg, then submerged up to my waist, but still felt nothing. The quasi floor had started moving in waves, like a bowl of jello. This was almost too much, but I had gone in up to my neck, and suddenly everything was as black as night. Was I free-falling, had I come up under a ledge or what?

I had inflated my BC to ascend, and when I popped out, my buddy had told me that the blackness flowed off my head like paint. It was spooky."

This is what Dr Steffi Schwabe originally wrote of her encounter with the first chemical layer, diving into what was to become known as the Black Hole of Andros. It's unique. Among the many famous blue holes of the Bahamas, which are collapsed entrances to prehistoric cave systems since flooded when sea-levels rose at the end of the last Ice Age, the Black Hole of Andros had intrigued the geologist, soft rock sedimentary petrologist and geomicrobiologist. It was different.

She and her husband, the famous cave diver Rob Palmer, had known about this black hole for years. They'd seen it from aerial photographs. At more than 300 m (100 ft) across it was big enough to be seen from space, but there was no way of getting there until much later after Rob's death, in a leisure diving accident far away in Egypt, when Steffi found access to a small seaplane.

That was because their targeted destination was in an area of the Bahamian outback, on Andros, the biggest island in the Bahamas archipelago. It was a place that no humans had ever visited, where the land surface was nothing but mud in places several metres deep. You couldn't walk or drive on it and you certainly could not transport heavy diving equipment across it. Steffi must be credited as the first person to scuba dive in it.

The question that intrigued the scientist in her, was that whatever developed a black hole such as this, was obviously tending to remain stable for very long periods of time, in parts possibly as long ago as 3.5 billion years.

But what lay beyond this black layer? She began to question the wisdom of attempting to pass down into it but the scientist within her put her well-being to one side.

"I asked myself, would it matter? The answer was no. I only hoped that I would survive to tell someone about it."

Sure enough, below this dark part, the water was crystal clear and yet below it another false floor. This was a purple-to-red colour. It had a jelly-like appearance. She was diving in some stupendous chemical cocktail that might have looked as spectacular as anything that a Bahamian barman could concoct, only not quite as appetising. It was certainly a unique environment and once she had made it back to the surface, her intention was to return as soon as she could.

However, access continued to be a problem and she had to wait a long time for another opportunity. This came when the producer of an Australian film company that was travelling around the world filming unusual things under water, suggested to her that they came to the Bahamas to film a sequence around the famous blue holes.

When she found out that their vessel came equipped with a Bell Ranger helicopter, she "thought all her Christmases had come at once". She persuaded them to do a sequence filming the black hole as well.

Two other people went with her. They were Cheryl Main, who had expertise in the study of algae, which she thought would be useful, and her boyfriend David, a surveyor who surveyed the black hole. She had planned for seven days of sampling.

After filming in some of the famous blue holes they took the helicopter and flew the 23 km (14 miles) inland to get to the black hole. It was at this point that Steffi discovered she only had two days to complete her work because of the financial constraints associated with several helicopter journeys. Steffi decided to make camp at the black hole rather than be flown back and forth, even though the Bahamian sun was brutally hot and there was little in the way of shelter beyond what they could rudely construct.

The area around the black hole was a nightmare of a swamp with mangrove and poisonwood growing in the mush. Even the limestone border of the hole was a brittle honeycomb of rock that formed razor sharp edges. It was a harsh environment above the hole, let alone in it, and she was intent on diving it again.

Steffi had a hydrolab that could measure geochemical parameters such as dissolved oxygen, temperature, pH, salinity and depth. She wanted to try to investigate the black layer before she dived into it.

She hooked the lab up to her computer. She watched the data move across the screen and suddenly saw the dissolved-oxygen level drop to nearly zero.

Something was consuming the oxygen at that level. It was the level where she had measured the depth of the black layer last time. It probably contained a very high level of hydrogen sulphide, one of the most poisonous substances known to man. What she failed to notice was the temperature reading, 37°C (99°F), and the low pH reading that indicated an acid environment. Her curiosity was overwhelming. She prepared to dive and was soon passing down through that black layer. It was her second visit to this unique place.

Scientific experiments were set up, samples taken for later analysis and other nearby holes investigated too. Dr Schwabe's efforts have resulted in the recent knowledge that the water in black holes appears black because of the metre-thick microbial layer, which lies at around 18–19 m (60 ft), dividing the oxic low-salinity water at the top, from denser anoxic saline water.

Analysis of her purple samples revealed that they had discovered a novel species of bacteria. In October 2003 it was officially named *Allocromatium palmeri* after her late husband, Rob. He was the first person to describe the Andros enigma in his book, *Deep into Blue Holes*, and as he had tried for nearly 20 years to reach this site, Dr Schwabe and her research colleague Dr Rod Herbert at Dundee, agreed that Rob should receive that honour.

Other samples were still being analysed. NASA's Johnson Space Centre in Houston had invited Dr Schwabe to apply for a summer fellowship to examine the rest of the samples in its state-of-the-art astrobiology laboratory, where she hoped that more amazing scientific discoveries would be made. You can read more about it in Steffi Jutta Schwabe's book, *Living in Darkness*.

Steffi had put the black hole on the scientific map but it was Paul Rose, making a big budget BBC series called *Oceans*, that brought it to the attention of a wider public.

Preparing an expedition to film there, he knew access was going to be an expensive problem to solve and was a bit suspicious that Steffi Schwabe, who was passionate about the biology of the hole, had only dived it twice in almost a decade.

The logistics overcome by helicopter, the BBC production team soon arrived at the site. They found it a very unpleasant place to be. Handling heavy diving gear was difficult because the soft terrain made setting up anything a difficult balancing act. Paul Rose takes up the story:

"The first part of our dive felt like many freshwater dives – cool, clear, green tinted water with us cruising down a steep rock all on the descent. We soon lost sight of the wall and at 17 m (55 ft) came on to the top of a dense dark-brown layer that looked exactly like the muddy bottom. I could not feel the layer and the top moved in thick clouds. We slowed our descent to study the layer and immediately felt the water get hot. Not just pleasantly warmer, but hot, an unhealthy 'get out of there' hot.

Within a few seconds the visibility went to zero. It was impossible to read my gauges and the only way I knew my torch was on was to hold it against my mask.

I was almost overwhelmed by a sudden blast of the smell of rotten eggs, which made no sense. You usually can't smell anything under water because your nose is inside the mask. In this case I could smell the bacteria in the layer because the chemicals were absorbed into the skin and I could smell them via my sinuses. I was being permeated with chemicals."

As Paul's diving team went deeper they suffered an even stronger attack on their olfactory senses. They passed down through the purple layer and came out into some reassuringly clear water, but of course no natural light penetrated. They found their way by the light from their lamps. They were now swimming in water that dated back through eons of time.

"What appeared to be a ceiling above us was black with bright green holes in it where we had come through surrounded by the strange red, purple layer underneath.

There was no avoiding it, we had to go back up through the layer and I needed to experience it again just to check that the assault on my senses was correct. Sure enough the visibility went to zero in the red, purple, smelly super-hot layer that came first, followed by the green smelly layer and then the wonderful cool, clear, life-giving fresh water at 17 m (55 ft)."

At the surface, Paul noted the chemical effect on the chrome surfaces of their equipment. He spotted their safety diver throwing up in the weeds. Tooni, his co-presenter and fellow diver, had toothache and their cameraman had a sore throat and felt ill. The strangest effect was on Paul himself. His hair had gone a weird gold colour.

THE OFFICER DIVER

A Royal Navy officer wants to be a naval diver and is regarded with deep suspicion by the petty officer charged with training him.

In later life, Lieutenant Commander (RN retired) David Sisman looked like the archetypal, retired Royal Naval officer. He was tall and frightfully well spoken with a protruding Adam's apple. He was also charming and erudite. His consuming passion was diving and he was one of the original founder members of the British Sub-Aqua Club. However, he'd originally learned to dive in the Navy and had eventually commanded a group of RN divers.

Later, as a diving club instructor, he often regaled his listeners with tales from Senior Service days and was sometimes quite derogatory about the men under his charge.

He enjoyed suggesting that if a sailor was obviously not clever enough to operate a mop, he'd be recommended to be a clearance diver. He was fond of telling how he'd do his best to keep his men diving healthily.

"Didn't you come up a bit too quickly? Aren't you concerned you might damage your brain?" he'd ask.

"What?"

"Oh, never mind."

David Sisman was also self-deprecating in the extreme. He was keen to tell that unplanned things can happen under water, especially in the very poor visibility encountered in British harbours. Related to this, his favourite anecdote was about himself and his baptism with a Royal Navy diving unit.

As a smart young officer he'd applied to be a diver and joined a diving unit where he reported to, and was met with, enormous suspicion by the Cockney chief petty officer in charge of training. This was a rough and ready man used to dealing with the lower ranks, and gentleman officers didn't usually become divers.

Not only that, but David Sisman made the mistake of professing to already have some basic diving skills, so the CPO decided to give him a simple test, a task under water in the dock.

"Sir, you officers never listen to instructions, so I'm going to ask you to repeat after me every single instruction I give you. Not only that, but when I say 'left'. I want you to repeat the instruction waving your left hand; when I say 'right', I want you to do the same with your right."

Sisman sighed and went along with this tedious charade.

"You will climb down the ladder fixed to the harbour wall to a depth of nine feet, where you will find a saw tied on the left-hand side."

The young officer carefully and precisely repeated what he had been told but forgot to wave his left hand. They started again.

"You will climb down the ladder fixed to the harbour wall to a depth of nine feet, where you will find a saw tied on the left-hand side."

This time he got it correct, waving his left hand as he spoke. The CPO then went on to tell him that on the right-hand side he would find a metal bar attached. He was to take the saw and cut through the metal bar, removing it.

The young officer listened sentence by sentence, repeating the instructions as he went and waving the appropriate hand. He found the whole rigmarole quite tiresome and demeaning, but he went along with it. What could be so difficult about climbing down a ladder, untying a saw and cutting off a metal bar?

The final instruction was, once the job was completed, to climb back up the ladder on to the dockside.

Equipped to dive in naval standard dress with brass helmet, David Sisman made his way to the top of the ladder, confident that he would soon have this basic task completed and be able to move on to something a bit more complex. He wore a safety rope tied around him with a bowline that was fed out by a man acting as the tender to the diver, while another manhandled his air hose.

Holding tightly to the side rails of the ladder, he stepped carefully backwards on to the first rung and slowly made his way down. The ladder was slimy and the diving equipment was heavy so he was careful not to make a fool of himself by slipping. The chief petty officer stood waiting at the top, regarding the officer and would-be diver with a critical eye.

Soon David's head was submerged and at this point he appreciated that the visibility afforded by water in a dockyard amounted to absolutely nothing at all. It was exceedingly murky down there. Nevertheless he continued to feel his way carefully down the ladder until his left hand came across the saw, tied on loosely as promised. He grasped it and wrenched it away. Now all he had to do was feel around for the metal bar. The conditions in the water weren't pleasant but he was under no time constraint so he decided to move cautiously until he found it.

It didn't take long. He soon got to work with the saw, cutting away. The naval diving equipment he was using can be quite constricting and he began to work up a sweat inside his suit. The thick rope that passed around his torso was getting in the way, too. The metal bar was probably about an inch thick and it was taking him longer than he expected to cut through it, but he persevered.

Finally, the saw made its last pass and the metal bar was cut through. The surprised young officer then fell off the ladder to dangle at the end of the safety rope. Instead of the intended metal bar, he'd managed to cut through the rung of the ladder he'd been standing on.

As a group of matelots helped his tender to haul him up on the rope out of the water from where he had been left floundering, the chief petty officer observed dryly, "Officers! They never listen to the instructions."

THE VOYAGES OF THE
LADY JENNY V

The doyen of diving liveaboard last century provided endless tales of daring and disaster. This
is just one.

One of a pair of Rhine river cruisers built in Bremen in 1936 for
the leaders of Germany, the *Lady Jenny V*, ended her days as
a support platform for expeditionary diving trips in the Red
Sea. The final owner, millionaire-engineer Tony Turner, had made his
money variously from inventing invalid carriages, lawnmowers at the
end of hydraulic arms used to cut the grass on the embankments of
motorways and, more recently, wood-chipping machines. He was not
a diver, but one thing led to another and he ended up operating his
private yacht, the *Lady Jenny V*, as a pioneering diving liveaboard.

The 20-year period from the start of the 1980s when she cruised this
harsh environment was eventful to say the least, and one day someone
will collate these events into a book and call it "The Voyages of the
Lady Jenny V". For example, in one six-month period during 1992, the
vessel was shot at three times while off the coasts of different countries
and the crew were arrested in another. In the meantime this author has

the problem of selecting just one story, which is difficult only because something remarkable happened every single day.

The *Lady Jenny V* had various crew. Nobody got paid much so it was more of a hobby job to work on her than a career decision, and few stayed for long. Notable crewmembers variously included people like Keith Cavendish, a diving survivor from the Piper Alpha oil platform disaster, and diving book author Lawson Wood. The passengers were equally interesting and included at times famous actors, novelists and film directors; even Leni Riefenstahl who'd known the vessel when it was newly built in Nazi Germany, and SAS soldier Charlie Cooke who'd swung in through a window of the Iranian embassy in Piccadilly one famous day, wearing a hood and firing a machine rifle. All those who were notable in the world's diving industry had journeyed on her at some time.

Many of the established dive sites visited by the burgeoning Egyptian diving industry today were first discovered by those who worked on the *Lady Jenny V*, but she was not an ideal vessel for diving.

Her original and enormously powerful Mercedes Benz engines were removed and replaced by more economic Detroit diesels. This made space for eight more berths below decks. Her skinny steel hull was originally built for the speed that these later engines could no longer provide and she was less than stable. Heavy equipment, her crane, her generators, the diving compressor and even the long saloon table, all fitted thoughtlessly to her starboard side, meant she travelled at a quirky angle. She was also difficult for divers to get on and off.

That all considered, this very elderly and somewhat unreliable vessel provided a base for dive trips that might be considered very risky by today's travel industry, or the height of adventure for those that booked her. At that time she was thought to be the doyen of diving liveaboards.

For one long, six-year period that was unusual simply for their tenacity in the face of adversity, the boat was run by the same English couple. He had been a dive guide in the Sudan, and he and his glamorous and bodacious blonde wife had been friends with Hans and Lotte Hass. They looked to be ideal for the job.

This may not have been entirely true. A boat becomes a small community of people for whom the captain must be the chief. It can also become a dictatorial fiefdom. Away from normality for long periods, people can develop private worlds of their own with a sometimes strange perception of how things are.

One regular passenger, an eminent diving doctor, once described the captain's wife as being totally sexy, beautiful and charming in port, but "she tended to turn into a three-headed monster once they lost sight of land".

Battling with a vessel and its equipment that was long past its sell-by date and with no reliable supply line, the husband, the ship's captain, looked perpetually angry. Then there was the parrot. The wife had a pet cockatoo. Sometimes it appeared to the passengers that the boat was run entirely for the parrot's benefit.

Each April, the *Lady Jenny V* would leave Egyptian waters and head south past the Sudan, Eritrea and over to the Yemen, ending up 2414 km (1500 miles) south at Djibouti before setting off back north, diving the reefs and wrecks on the way. For many passengers, this represented the diving trip of a lifetime.

In those days nobody bothered with paperwork, although they should have. There were no permissions ever issued to operate the *Lady Jenny V* other than around the immediate environs of the Ras Mohammed marine park at the southern tip of the Sinai. The crew simply stocked the vessel with supplies and took their chances. I don't think the paying passengers ever fully appreciated this.

In 1991, the vessel and all on board, were arrested by the Eritrean People's Liberation Front while trying to enter a military area in the Dahlak islands. The passengers and crew were taken into the port of Massawa. The beautiful Red Sea port, originally built in the style of an Italian wedding cake, had been bombed daily for 17 years by the Russian-supplied Ethiopian Air Force. Nothing was left standing. From there the crew were transported to Asmara where they were held for an additional and worrying six weeks, although the passengers were soon released. The Eritreans had only just won a war of independence from the Ethiopians and the country was littered with burnt-out Russian-made tanks. The *Lady Jenny V* was confiscated.

Tony Turner, the owner, travelled in person to Massawa and per-suaded the authorities there to repatriate the vessel. A year later, during the following southern Red Sea cruise, and after being fired on in a friendly manner by an Eritrean gunboat, she entered Massawa harbour again and various Eritrean government dignitaries came on board for a meal, including the then Minister of Tourism.

After reading the tale told by the previous year's crew in the British press, the captain of the gunboat who had originally arrested the vessel was keen to tell his own side of the story. We know his name variously as Johnnie or Jerry, but it had originally been reported as Jerry Can. We never found out his family name, but he was the epitome of an Eritrean freedom fighter, educated as a child in Germany with good linguistic skills. He spoke English without a trace of an accent.

"The *Lady Jenny V* was seen to enter the main lagoon in the Dahlak islands. This was the headquarters of the EPLF Navy and was a restricted area. We had only just finished 17 years of war and any strange vessel was regarded with suspicion.

I informed the captain of the *Lady Jenny V* of this. He told me they wanted to dive on the wreck of one of the Italian warships that were known to have been sunk in the lagoon during World War II. I told them that this was impossible. It was a military restricted area. The vessel left.

That afternoon it was back again, and again I informed its captain that this was a restricted area and he should leave or we might need to arrest them. Again they left.

It was unbelievable that they tried to return a third time under cover of darkness. At this point I went over to arrest them and boarded with a group of armed fighters. I would have taken them into Massawa and maybe held them up for a couple of days, but the captain's wife, that woman with the parrot, decided to attack me in front of my men. She pulled off my futa (a traditional skirt worn by men) and humiliated me. It then got worse. The captain (later disputed by the Englishman who insists he would never have said such a racist thing), then called me a 'third-world, nomadic, black bastard'. This meant that I was forced to arrest them and send them to Asmara. We Eritreans are not nomadic!"

SCARY TIMES IN
THE RED SEA

Two frightening events that happened to a diving liveaboard operating in the Red Sea, off the coast of what were unfriendly countries.

E ven in the mid-nineties the southern Red Sea could represent a very scary place, not just because of its remoteness but because of the political and military unrest that was common at that time in that part of the world.

The *Lady Jenny V*, now ancient and faltering, still made the regular annual trip down its length, travelling 2414 km (1500 miles) picking up and dropping off passengers from different ports, passengers that were prepared to put up with a bit more than simple adventure. They dived the sites of Egypt, the Sudan, Eritrea, the Yemen and Djibouti on the way.

One dive guide recalls sitting in the inflatable pick-up boat, waiting for divers from Keighley Sub-Aqua Club to complete a night dive, when he heard what he thought was the outboard motor misfiring. They were used to all sorts of regular mechanical breakdowns and he wasn't surprised.

The Scottish deckhand, Patrick, said it wasn't the outboard. Then they saw a red flare – it made its way weakly into the night sky before falling back.

"It's someone letting off old flares at the shore," the dive guide surmised and shone his powerful diving torch towards where the flare had originated.

The image of six army squaddies in a kneeling position and taking aim at him will stay with him forever.

Bullets whistled around them accompanied by the pop of the Kalashnikovs. The dive guide held the lamp over his heart, reasoning that they seemed to be such lousy shots that if they aimed for the lamp, they'd surely miss him.

Meanwhile the divers started to surface, eager to talk about what they'd seen under water. Adrenalin was flowing in the inflatable. The guys dragged each surfacing diver, somewhat surprised, into the boat fully kitted. They soon got the idea and 18 divers were stacked in a boat designed to take a maximum of ten, but nobody was complaining. Those at the bottom of the pile thought they had reason to be grateful.

Back on the *Lady Jenny V*, the incumbent captain, Mike Archer, was waiting. He had seen what was happening. The engines were running and as soon as the frightened divers were safely on board, the inflatable was taken in tow and they got out of there.

The elderly lady, the *Lady Jenny V*, tottered on and later was to be found down in the far south near the border between Djibouti and Eritrea.

Some of her passengers had known the vessel when it was younger and the passenger list by now included the very famous "Shark Lady" Dr Eugenie Clarke. The eminent American ichthyologist was famous as a young woman for personally persuading Sadat, the then President of Egypt, to make the now famous diving area around Ras Mohammed into a marine park. She had a long-standing relationship with the Red Sea and had a long-standing relationship with the vessel too; although both had by now seen better days.

Genie wanted to dive in a particular bay. To Mike Archer's knowledge, no one had ever dived there before and he was eager to please such an important guest. She and her similarly highly qualified ichthyologist buddy, John Pohli, were dropped off in the inflatable with instructions that they were to be picked up exactly one hour later. Mike took the *Lady Jenny V* and stood off to wait.

During that time Mike noticed a number of vehicles starting to gather on the beach. These were not the cars of curious tourists. In this part of the world few civilians even had cars. They were military vehicles. Soon they were receiving a radio message that the captain of the white motor yacht was to come ashore for interrogation.

This was not a time to cut and run. Mike had two very important divers under water and no way of communicating with them.

He prevaricated for as long as he could but time was running out. Eugenie Clarke and her buddy were soon due to surface in the bay between the vessel and the beach, now filling with military vehicles.

Eventually, he made a great play of coming ashore in the inflatable. Kenny MacDonald, the ship's engineer, had the engines running and was waiting in the wheelhouse. They had a plan and it was risky.

Mike Archer sat in the inflatable while the deckhand drove it very slowly towards the shore. He said that he tried to look like Captain Bligh being driven by a subordinate.

They motored slowly. Everything depended on Eugenie and her buddy being disciplined enough to surface on time as arranged. The divers knew nothing of the drama unfolding above them.

Exactly on cue their heads broke the surface. The two guys in the boat didn't waste time in feeling relieved. They dragged the divers unceremoniously over the tubes of the inflatable and turned, heading back at full speed to the *Lady Jenny V*.

As soon as they were alongside, helping hands pulled the two elderly divers up on to the aft deck, the deckhand secured the painter to the long line with which they could tow the inflatable, and Kenny MacDonald put the vessel into reverse, opening up the Detroit diesels to their fullest revolutions.

The old girl shook and shuddered as she went backwards faster than she was supposed to do. Mike by now had run up to the wheelhouse and thrown the helm over hard so that she swung her nose out into the open sea.

Full throttle forwards and she was soon doing her maximum speed of ten knots, which is not very fast at all.

By now they had seen that the armed men had given chase in a huddle of flat-bottomed dories. Mike turned to the north. The Red Sea is famous for its vicious, short, choppy waves, the result of a prevailing northwesterly desert wind.

The *Lady Jenny V*'s slim hull was built from good German steel, even if it was a long time ago. Water from the waves they ploughed through poured over the prow, washing everything before it down the decks. The passengers huddled in the saloon while the old motor yacht plunged forwards. She wasn't fast but she was tough.

The dories weren't making any headway in this sort of sea and they soon gave up. They had escaped!

There is a postscript to this story. Three or four weeks later, Mike was skippering the *Lady Jenny V* and moored up off one of the outer islands of the Seven Brothers that mark the junction of the Red Sea with the Gulf of Aden.

Over the top of the island came a low-flying, military helicopter that hovered ahead of them. The crew waved to the pilot with a slight feeling of apprehension.

Again adrenalin was running high when the pilot fired a long burst from two 30 mm cannons that hit the water passing either side of the motor yacht's narrow hull. They weren't sure if he'd missed or had intended to simply make an expensive gesture, but the helicopter turned and flew away, presumably to get more ammunition. The *Lady Jenny V*'s anchor was raised in a hurry and she headed out into the international sea-lanes. The helicopter returned and lined up once more but the pilot obviously chose not to break international law and did not fire again. Mike Archer decided enough was enough.

FANTASY ISLAND ONE

When a group of experienced divers and diving journalists accept an invitation, things may not be as originally promised.

It was an invitation to stay at a millionaire's resort, a luxury hideaway for divers set on a remote island in the Outer Hebrides. The invitation included a copy of the menu from the resort's restaurant. It looked too good to be true and it was.

Five people accepted the invitation. Who wouldn't? All they had to do was to make their own way to Castlebay on the island of Barra and it was going to be luxurious pampering from then on. Two came from Holland, two from England and George Brown, himself a Highlander, represented the British Sub-Aqua Club.

Alarm bells started to ring after they met up with the proprietor, Ben Dodd, on the jetty at Castlebay. Their transport from then on was to be a retired Atlantic 21 inshore lifeboat. Now, this was a very fast and seaworthy small boat designed to make retrieval of people from the water easy. It did this by having no transom and a flooding hull. Once it came to rest, it settled down in the water on its inflatable sponsons or tubes to allow the lifeboat men to easily drag a person from the water onboard. At this time they would themselves be a couple of feet deep in water but they were dressed for that.

Observing the boat, the visitors wisely decided to don their diving drysuits for the journey of about 30 km (19 miles) to the resort that was based on the island of Berneray, the most southern and remotest in the island chain. They then planned to load the bags with their diving equipment into the boat, while keeping all their dry clothes in one bag perched at the top of the pile and hopefully out of the water.

They were somewhat surprised when Ben Dodd turned up with a pile of old mattresses. He intended to ship them over at the same time, until it was pointed out that it would take months to dry them out afterwards. At this point Trevor Woodfine strolled by. He was a Geordie working as a diver doing boat repairs in the harbour.

He quietly offered the opinion to one of the visitors that they would be crazy to go out to sea with Mr Dodd because he patently didn't know what he was doing. Trevor was persuaded to come with them and take the helm.

The Atlantic 21 was very fast if wet, and they soon arrived at Berneray. The last item on the menu they had received with the invitation had been "fresh fish caught at the jetty", but they were surprised to find that the jetty, built by Robert Stevenson in 1833, had been washed away about a hundred years before they got there. More alarm bells rang when two young people came down to meet them and asked if they had any food because they hadn't eaten for two days. One was Mr Dodd's sister, Pippa.

Luckily, the canny Highlander George Brown had suspected things might not be as promised and had the foresight to visit a grocery store before they had set off from Castlebay. The carrier bag's contents proved to be a lifesaver.

Everything had to be swum ashore in a rough sea, including the all-important bag of dry clothes. It was at this point that Mr Dodd revealed that he had no way of filling the scuba tanks that the five had brought with them, so Trevor headed back to Castlebay to do it. That left them all without a radio and in the days before mobile phone coverage, no means of communication to the outside world. They had to trust that Trevor would make it back all right the next morning.

They made their way up the steep hill to the abandoned lighthouse keeper's accommodation at its top. The lighthouse had been automatic for some years and it turned out that Mr Dodd had done little more than break in to the disused buildings. There was no sign of the luxury promised.

It was getting quite chilly as night set in, so they busied themselves chopping up some floorboards to feed an ancient kitchen range on which they hoped to heat some of the precious food they had brought with them. Others chopped up floorboards to feed to open grates that were the only source of heat for the bedrooms. There was no danger of carbon monoxide poisoning thanks to a good flow of air through the broken windows.

So there were no diving facilities, no compressor, no luxury accommodation, only the food they had bought with them by chance and no functioning bathrooms. When one of the ladies asked for the facilities, she was presented with a spade and it was suggested that she went outside in the cool autumn breeze and attempt to dig a suitable hole in the hard granite surface.

Electricity was supplied by one tiny generator. Well, that was the intention but it seemed that fuel for this was scarce, so the meagre light from a handful of candles was all they could see by.

When accused of being misleading, Mr Dodd retorted that everyone was being very negative. Somehow, he was living a fantasy. When it was suggested that there was no food, he disagreed and said there was plenty, produced a shotgun and suggested someone went outside and shot one of the many sheep grazing on the island.

The group spent a cold and uncomfortably dark night, sleeping in their diving undersuits in beds with legs now balanced on the exposed joists where there were once floorboards. They were relieved to see Trevor Woodfine return at first light in the Atlantic 21 with their tanks filled ready for diving.

The Atlantic 21 is arguably, the finest small rescue boat of its type ever built. Strong, self-righting and with fully submersible outboards, it took the unkind seas around the islands in its long stride. But as a dive boat it wasn't ideal. With no transom, the interior flooded when stationary and left them wading around looking for the smaller items of their kit, hoping they hadn't been swept out the aft when the boat took off, which it did, when asked, without hesitation.

Barrahead lighthouse on Berneray is set atop a stupendously high granite cliff. Ben Dodd had promised they could be the first to dive the Barrahead Wall, but it transpired that the water beneath the cliff was a mere 12 m (39 ft) deep and strewn with nothing more interesting than a few boulders.

Trevor proved to be the hero of the trip, travelling back to Castlebay each night and returning the next day with the diving tanks filled. However, this rather limited the number of dives they could do and by the third day they abandoned the whole project.

As a postscript to the story, Pippa, Mr Dodd's sister, later became a lawyer and found herself working in London with the sister of one of the ladies of the group. When the subject of diving came up and the connection became apparent, she revealed that she too had been taken in by her brother and was still under the illusion that, as she walked across the cobbled yard of the disused lighthouse keeper's cottages, there would be a warm meal and a hot shower awaiting her inside. Evidently, she had not spoken to her brother since getting off his Fantasy Island.

FANTASY ISLAND TWO

An experienced group of divers and diving journalists are invited to visit an island dive camp in the Yemen in mid-summer but they should have known better.

If the Outer Hebrides in autumn were cold, an island called Antufash in the Farasans, south of Saudi Arabia and off the coast of Yemen, in mid-summer was hotter than hell. A group of experienced British divers and diving journalists were invited on an educational trip to a diving resort, a dive camp, based there.

When it was suggested to the tour operator that invited them that it would be unacceptably hot, he replied that they had planted trees around the campsite and built a micro-climate. He also promised that there were air-conditioned tents. They should have known better. It was wishful thinking.

Unusually, they were asked to take their own scuba tanks with them, which proved something of a problem at the check-in desk for Yemenia, the state airline of the Yemen. Notwithstanding, the group finally made it to Hodeida, the Red Sea port of the Yemen.

The group drove from the airport to Al Luhayyah. It's the sort of town that had suffered an earthquake but none of the locals had noticed. Everywhere, people were living in what appeared to be collapsed buildings. One of the group sought privacy in one build-ing and disturbed a colony of bats that flew out like a swarm of bees into the brightly lit sky only to be dramatically picked off by a group of marauding eagles.

Here the group strode out into the fetid shallow water of an estuary to join two small and primitive open boats in rather poor condition that awaited them to make the final leg of the journey to the island of Antufash. These boats had precious little freeboard once loaded with the Brits, who were somewhat larger than the locals.

Once they arrived after a couple of hours at sea, they immediately noticed no sign of any trees on this sun-blasted sandspit. The promised micro-climate proved to be a fantasy. The Italian resident manager of the dive camp asked them how long they were intent on staying. When told it was ten days, he remarked that they would go crazy after seven. The wild-eyed Moroccan chef said he was already out of his head. Things didn't look too promising.

The ten visitors shared five simple 2-man tents. These tents were barely cooled by ordinary electric fans that blew the deep, fine, soft sand from the floor over their beds and bodies sticky with sweat. It made sleep almost impossible. Things got worse. During the night, the little petrol-driven generator would run out of fuel and the fans would stop.

Fresh water was supplied in two 5-gallon jerry cans that were ferried each day from Al Luhayyah. It didn't go far between the ten visitors. Dehydration was a real risk, so washing in the mean supply from the improvised shower was out of the question. Underwater cameras and equipment had to be neglected and left salty from the sea.

Daytime air temperatures were so high someone remarked that walk-ing down the steep white sandy beach to the water's edge was like climbing up a hill. When the sun set, there was a moment of respite before the air became black with ravenous mosquitoes and everyone had to retreat to the safety of their hot little tents.

The sea gave no respite from the heat. Near the shore, it was warmer than body temperature. That part of the Red Sea is set on a great bank of sand known as the Farasan Bank. There is precious little coral to speak of. There was no marine life to see near the surface save for a million red crabs that marched out of the water and unstoppably through their camp each dawn and dusk.

Peter Rowlands, one of the visitors, recounted years later that at 30 m (100 ft) deep, the water was still as hot as 32°C (90°F). The divers found they had to go as deep as 40 m (130 ft) to see any fish life at all. This meant long boat rides to get to deep water and, breathing compressed air under water, long decompression stops. This may have been inadvisable so far from any medical help should things have gone wrong, but one diver observed at the time, that at least during these long mandatory hangs in the shallower water they weren't getting sunburnt.

Sunburn was a big problem. Without any cover for the boats to provide shade during these journeys to and from dive sites, the British divers needed to wrap their heads in wet towels simply to stay alive.

After a week, the resort manager announced there had been a double booking and he needed some volunteers to give up the diving expedition and spend the rest of their trip in Sa'ana, the capital of the Yemen. He got all his volunteers almost without exception and they escaped from another Fantasy Island.

THE OLD MAN
OF THE SEA

Old age may take its toll but it also gives an insight into diving, only earned with time.

Many divers may know Stan Waterman only as an older man, but he didn't start life that way. He has spent the greater part of his life under water and of course much of that has been as an elder statesman of diving. As an octogenarian he was still diving and celebrated his eightieth birthday diving Costa Rica's Cocos Island, a place not known for easy conditions. He then went on to have a second birthday party shortly after at Rangiroa, in French Polynesia, where he dived with the sharks and his friends Peter Benchley, the author of *Jaws*; pioneering 3D underwater wildlife film maker Howard Hall, and famous shark wranglers, Australians Ron and Valerie Taylor. In the introduction to Stan's first autobiography *Sea Salt*, Howard Hall remembers how Stan coped in the roaring currents and schooling sharks of the Tiputa Pass.

"Stan made his move across the current (through the massed sharks) at the last possible moment, kicking ferociously. His timing had been perfect. As he swam up to the others and me, Stan, filled with enthusiasm, pumped his fist, rolled his eyes and yelled 'Wow!' loudly through his regulator mouthpiece."

Stan was famous for working with Ron and Valerie Taylor filming aggregated, oceanic white-tip sharks that were feeding off whale carcasses for Peter Gimbel's extraordinary award-winning documentary *Blue Water White Death*. Along with Chuck Nicklin and Al Giddings, he was an underwater cameraman during the filming of Peter Benchley's story *The Deep*. This blockbusting 1977 movie starred Nick Nolte, Robert Shaw and Jacqueline Bisset.

Years later, he came to Britain to attend an annual dive show and while there, he gave a presentation. Predictably, it was oversubscribed and the audience were standing in the aisles even though the presentation hall had a huge seating capacity.

The dive show carried on over two days. On the evening of the first day he took dinner with the show organisers.

"What an incredible audience," the great man commented. "I've never seen so many people turn up for one of my talks." "Normally, I'm happy if a dozen or so show," he added modestly. "However, I must say that they were an earnest bunch. They didn't seem to laugh very easily."

Then someone offered a reason.

"Stan," he said, "you gave a very interesting talk and showed some pretty slides, but it was all about the wonders of coral reefs. These people know you as the famous cameraman who shot *The Deep*. They want to know what it was like to spend all day with Jacqui Bisset wearing a wet T-shirt!"

The great man gave it some thought and, as with all great men, he was modest enough to consider the input from a third person. Next day his presentation was completely different. He told stories associated with working on the film. The tale remembered here is recorded in his autobiography *Sea Salt*.

In the shooting script, the lady star of the movie was to be filmed surfacing from a dive by the stern of a small boat that was used in the story. This was to be filmed both from the main vessel (or production boat) as well as from water level. The three underwater cameramen decided to shoot the scene with their cameras "over and under" the surface of the water, with their underwater camera lenses half in and half out. They did this by floating their heavy 35 mm motion picture Arriflex cameras on inflatable rafts that could be adjusted for buoyancy so that they were just right. The production boat carried around 20 other assorted members of the film crew.

The cameramen heard the command to "turn over", switched their cameras to run and ducked down under water to look through their viewfinders. At the same time, the surface film cameras on the production boat began to roll.

The director called "action" and on that word Jacqueline Bisset swam down under the water and surfaced, as required by the script, next to the ladder of the small boat. She looked wet but divine. At precisely the same moment, an unplanned object floated into view between her and the running cameras. Jacqui stopped acting and her attention became fixed on this object. Stan told how he brought his head up from the water to hear the director going apoplectic with rage.

"They all stared incredulously as a huge turd floated by."

Stan continued, "Some nerd in the camera-boat had gone below and used the head and flushed it at the precise moment of the call to action!"

Some years later, on his eightieth birthday, he was to be found under water at a dive site in Cocos called Alcyon. It's deep and subject to strong water movement and the surface of the Pacific Ocean above is unprotected from the wind. Starting to look a little frail because of his age, younger divers on the liveaboard vessel they used, were inclined to give the elderly gentleman advice. They forgot that with the absence of gravity under water, the years fell off him and his long experience outranked their youthful vigour.

Another diver, and the same man that had given him advice years previously at that dive show, returning late to the surface from deeper water, encountered him recording the activities of a tiny jawfish with his enormous underwater video camera, oblivious to a chaos of hammerhead sharks circling round his head. Stan had obviously seen enough sharks to last a lifetime. Agreeing that it was time to ascend, the two made their way over to the anchor line of the panga that was being used as a pick-up boat.

They ascended together slowly and paused at 6 m (20 ft) for a few minutes. The line snatched as the boat above them plunged and bucked on an uninviting sea. They looked up to see the occasional explosion of vomit from some of the other younger divers that waited in the boat above them. It obviously wasn't nice up there.

They broke the surface and the younger man dutifully let the older man climb up the boat ladder first. As he climbed, Stan paused for thought for a moment. He looked at the green faces of those that had been waiting and were now suffering the various and obviously debilitating stages of mal de mer. He turned back to the other diver who still floated below him next to the ladder.

"When you get to my age," he said with a somewhat mischievous and wry smile, "it's best to be the last one in the boat."

PART THREE

Deep Diving

THE *BRITANNIC*

The dive considered to be the Everest of technical diving is the one on the wreck of the *Britannic*, but Greek officialdom and corruption adds to the degree of difficulty.

S ister ship to the *Titanic* that so famously sank on its maiden voyage, the *Britannic* survived only to serve as a hospital ship during World War I. It was on its way to pick up casualties from the battle for Gallipoli when it sank in the Aegean Sea after hitting a mine in the Kea Channel. It was 21st November 1916.

This enormous vessel now lies at around 120 m (400 ft) deep in an area that is swept by strong currents and is home to a busy shipping lane. Divers must battle with the vagaries of the authorities to get permission to dive it, and then deal with the surface hazards that might be encountered before descending into a deep dark place that needs special diving techniques. They must also contend with the strong water movement between the wreck and the surface. The warm surface water is soon left behind for the relative chill of the deep. Similarly, the Greek sunshine only penetrates enough to give a gloomy blue light.

A team led by Cousteau was the first to dive it in 1975 but since then, there have been several expeditions to conquer the ultimate wreck dive.

The biggest problem diving at such a depth is one of gas planning. Divers use different mixes of gases to breathe at different depths in order to maximise their dive times and their ability to operate properly at extreme depth. The helium-based mixes can be hypoxic at shallower depths. In the same way, the oxygen in recreational breathing gases becomes poisonous at extreme depth. This means that divers using conventional scuba equipment need to take multiple tanks of gas with them and breathe from the appropriate one at any given depth. It also means long ascent times approaching several hours in order to make the staged decompression stops on the way up, allowing the body to off-gas and avoid the "bends". The sheer volumes of gas needed, with multiple tanks, become a logistical problem under water too.

The advent of the electronically controlled closed-circuit rebreather has alleviated some of these problems. The gas breathed is recirculated within the equipment, with the small amount of oxygen consumed automatically replenished, while the very poisonous carbon dioxide produced by the human body as a by-product of metabolism, is chemically removed. Closed-circuit rebreathers have made very deep dives more practical since a far smaller volume of gas is required to be carried by the diver. Even so, around 40 minutes on the wreck meant up to five-and-a-half hours under water allowing for a careful ascent time. However, adding technicalities can add problems as well as solutions.

"Shadow divers" John Chatterton and Richie Kohler made a History Channel television programme about the sinking of the *Titanic* in which they postulated that there was a design fault in the hull construction of the great ship that caused the vessel to break up at the surface after running aground on the iceberg. Part of their theory was that Harland and Wolff, the builders, knew about the defect and had corrected it when they later built the sister ships, the *Britannic* and the *Olympic*. The supposed fault was attributed to the shape of the expansion joints let into the hull that allowed the vessel to flex or "breathe" while she was under way. In order to support their theory, they needed video footage of details of the surviving hull of the *Britannic* and the possibly modified expansion joints. They led an underwater expedition in 2006 to obtain that footage with high-definition video cameras specifically constructed for the project by the Woods Hole Oceanographic Institute.

The team also needed to check if the watertight bulkhead doors had been left open, which might have been a clue to the *Britannic's* unexpectedly fast sinking after her hull was breached by the mine's explosion. After all, her propellers had still been turning as she went down, with fatal consequences for many already in the lifeboats.

The Greek authorities and the wreck's owner, Simon Mills, had insisted that only closed-circuit rebreathers were used so that no exhaled gas would cause degradation by oxidation of the structure of the wreck.

Martin Parker and Mike Etheridge were support divers and qualified to be part of the team, as the designer and chief test diver of the majority of closed-circuit rebreathers that were employed for the job. Other members of the group assembled for the task included Leigh Bishop, Carl Spencer, Mike Barnette, Eduardo Pavia, Mark Bullen, Mike Fowler, Evan Kovacs, Mike Pizzio and Frankie Pelegrino.

Despite being defrauded by the originally briefed, local shore manager, as well as having a second supply of cash stolen with violence from the member of the team carrying it back from the bank, a very unsuitable dive support vessel and poor quality local tanks, the expedition finally got positioned over the dive site.

Britannic lay towards its starboard side, covered in sponges, marine growth and discarded fishing nets. Every dive team was assigned tasks. Mike Etheridge and Martin Parker were to locate the maker's plate and the telephone in the crow's nest.

Mike Etheridge had been delayed arriving in Greece because he had been investigating a newly found wreck at 90 m (295 ft) deep off the coast of Cornwall.

After the poor conditions they were used to in the English Channel, both Brits recounted being blown away by the extremely clear visibility under water in the Aegean. They reckoned they could see 60 metres horizontally and once down at 60 m (200 ft) deep they could see the mighty vessel resting on its side like a model ship a further 60 metres below them. It was amazing. For the Brits it was "like diving in a swimming pool".

They found the steel plate where the brass maker's plate should have been, but it was gone. They looked in the debris below but couldn't find it and they had the same problem with the crow's nest telephone. That gave them a good excuse to go to the bottom and explore the bow section.

Martin Parker later said, "Looking back at the *Britannic* superstructure was an image that will live with me forever – fantastic to see so much of such a large wreck without swimming."

Since their failed attempt to reach the watertight doors on a previous expedition, Chatterton had been considering access via a fireman's tunnel. Chatterton and Kohler were soon deep on the sleeping giant and, passing under a fishing net that otherwise obstructed their route, left the blue gloom of daylight for the interior of the wreck.

After crawling through this long fireman's tunnel they were soon in the boiler room. Neither of them had remembered ever seeing such a large enclosed space under water before, but a wheelbarrow jammed in concreted silt in a narrow companionway, hindered their penetration. They had to abort the dive.

Meanwhile nearly all the team of divers were falling ill with severe stomach upsets from contaminated food and became unable to dive further. Those that had endured long periods of decompression in the water were looking particularly poorly – including John Chatterton.

This meant that the British support divers who had arrived later, accompanied by American Mike Barnette, were detailed to go down to video an expansion joint.

While the American slowly descended all the way down the shot-line, the two Brits had saved time by cutting across open blue water and swimming directly to where they thought one joint might be located. It took them only three minutes to descend from the surface before landing on the side of the hull.

They counted the portholes between funnel numbers two and three before locating what they were after. Mike Etheridge then got busy with a selection of chisels and a lump hammer, smashing off the heavy covering of goose barnacles to reveal the expansion joint properly. He found that the current pushing up over the side of the hull made it difficult for him to get a good purchase so he thrust a chisel through the rusting side of ship and wrapped one leg around its protruding handle.

Martin continued making a recording of details of the outside of the hull but the video camera had misted up in the middle of its image. He contrived to use the margins instead. They had swum half the length of the wreck but their dive had lasted only two hours and 20 minutes. Mike Barnette had mistakenly assumed they'd not found the expansion joint. Their bubble-count checked by the DAN doctor on-board the support vessel was the lowest of any of the divers on the expedition. It was only their second dive of the trip and the first actually on the wreck, but the project was then brought to an abrupt halt.

Every expedition since Cousteau's had been mired in a swamp of bureaucracy. Both the British and Greek governments needed to give simultaneous permissions to dive the wreck. The Greek Department of Antiquities was paranoid that the expedition might use the opportunity to search for other wrecks or antiquities. A Greek official on board the diving support vessel was continually suspicious of their intentions. He unilaterally decided that the divers were violating their government permit (written in Greek) by going inside the wreck, but the whole purpose of the expedition had been to examine the watertight doors as well as the expansion joints, so the expedition members knew this was not true. The expedition had already fallen victim to corruption, fraud and theft. Greek officialdom is not known for its honesty and it was suspected that this was yet another bizarre attempt to extort more money out of the expedition organisers.

By the following day the Greek police had arrested Chatterton and Kohler and frogmarched them away. The videotapes were seized. Luckily, they had the foresight to make duplicates beforehand. The main story is recorded in a chapter of Brad Matsen's *Titanic's Last Secrets*.

Four years later, Carl Spencer led a team of those thought at the time to be probably the top technical divers in the world, to dive the *Britannic* in order to film sequences for a National Geographic production.

He encountered technical problems with his closed-circuit rebreather at depth and needed to "bail out" to conventional open-circuit scuba in order to get back to the surface. There was some confusion between gas cylinders and, breathing an inappropriate gas, he sadly lost his life during the ascent. The loss of this popular character in the technical diving world has made many deep divers think again about what they do, and, like the conquest of Everest, it may be the ultimate achievement but dives on the *Britannic* will inevitably claim more lives in the future.

THE CALL OF THE WAH! WAH!

Some divers go very deep breathing air and for one it nearly ends in disaster.

In the early nineties a pioneering group of technical diving, agency trainers met up in the Bahamas for the launch of the Draeger rebreather. They were disappointed to find that it was intended for the novice end of the leisure diving market and not what they were expecting at all.

They decided to take a couple of days out and go for some serious blue water diving at the AUTEC buoy, moored in the deep water of the Tongue of the Ocean.

"It is approximately 23 m (75 ft) in diameter. It's big. You could have a party for a 100 people on top of this thing. When we did the second dive, we were out on its cable. The buoy is moored in 2000 m (7200 ft) of water. There is no bottom reference." This was how Bob Raimo later described it.

Some have denied the following ever happened but the story told here is abstracted from what Bob Raimo talked about with other divers at the time.

When asked how deep he wanted to go, Bob suggested he'd go as deep as he felt comfortable with. He said he was not there to set any personal or industry records: he was there to have a good time.

The others dived with single 80 (11.4-litre) cylinders as normally used for any leisure dive, but Bob thought that too risky with insufficient gas.

"I was very uncomfortable diving with a single 80 so I jury-rigged some telephone wire to another 80 stage bottle because I refused to go deep on a single 80. I wanted to at least have a back-up bottle."

On the first day they dived deep and Bob thought he was completely in control and fully capable of helping somebody else, which was his measurement of his comfort level. He reported feeling fine at 100 m (325 ft). He checked his gauges and stopped at 76 m (250 ft) on the way up in case anybody else needed air.

On the second day he made two big mistakes. He grabbed the weight belt from his rebreather configuration instead of the weight belt suitable for use with the conventional aluminium tanks he intended to use. This meant he had an extra 3.5 kg (8 lb) of lead on his belt.

Other experienced deep air divers were saying that one of the things that you need to be able to do if you're going to go deep, is to get down there fast and get out of there fast. The day before, Bob had noticed he couldn't keep up with those guys. When he said he "kinda floated down like he normally did" one of the others suggested that there was a lot of drag that way. He thought it was better to go down head first.

He never discussed before with any of them how they did it. None of them had gone to the Bahamas with any of this in mind. If he'd have known the week before he later said, he'd have brought some clips and hooks and stainless steel tank bands. "He'd have come ready to make real stage bottles, not telephone wire."

The dive went wrong.

They descended head first alongside the long, mooring cable as suggested. At around 100 m (330 ft) Bob looked at his depth gauge. He decided that was deep enough for him and waved his arm to signal he was levelling off. He started to inflate his BC (buoyancy control device) in order to hover at that depth.

"So, I'm inflating my BC and I'm going deeper and deeper... 348 feet, 350, my BC's full, 352, and I'm not feeling too happy. I went from feeling really good to feeling really 'narked'. This is where I made what I believe to be the second and almost fatal mistake. I kicked. I used my legs, which is the normal diver reaction. At that point, I just wanted to stop the descent. Not even to go up, just to stop."

The effort of kicking changed his metabolism. He reported that he went from being completely in control into a complete headspin.

"That one kick used so much O_2 and generated so much CO_2... and I was like, whoa, man, I got really messed up. And it happened again, and I went, whoa man... and thank God for that cable. (The massive cable that moored the buoy to the seabed far below.) I just reached out with my right hand and – ka-chink – barehanded. This cable had fish hooks on it and was encrusted with all kinds of shit. But believe me, I was so numb I didn't feel anything. I just grabbed on to this cable. I looked at my depth gauge again, and all the pixels were lit up on my screen."

By this time he had no idea how deep he was. He knew that he had fully inflated his BC and he wasn't going up. His first tank was only half-full with air by now so he decided to pull himself up the mooring cable. In the blue water, it would have been his only point of reference.

He began to pull himself up the cable. He must have passed other divers but he didn't recall it. One remembered Bob's eyes rolling up in his head, as if he were asleep.

"One thing that really scared me was this noise. When I couldn't read my gauges, I heard this noise – wah-wah-wah-wah – really loud. I didn't know what it was. When I heard the noise, I could not see my hand on the cable. All I could see was my gauge. I couldn't see anything else. Everything surrounding the gauge was black."

He became focused on not losing consciousness. He was determined to reach up to 30 m (100 ft) where he planned to stop ascending and pause to gather himself together emotionally and allow his body to decompress.

"You can't black out, you've gotta do deco," he kept telling himself. He recalled later that he felt he kept kicking as he pulled himself up the cable but he couldn't be sure. He had a very strong desire to live yet he recalled thinking that he could very easily have given up and died.

At around 50 m (164 ft) he became aware that the background was blue. He was regaining his senses and starting to see other divers again. He could by now read his gauges and things quickly returned to normal. A few prayers were offered and he swam on upwards to 12 m (40 ft) and another stop for further decompression.

He met up with one of the other divers in the shallows. When they got out of the water, Bob described to him what had happened on the dive. Another deep diver said that the noise was very typical. If someone hasn't heard that noise, then he hadn't been that deep on air.

Air is made up primarily of nitrogen and oxygen. Under sufficient pressure caused by depth, the nitrogen has a narcotic effect on the nervous system. Oxygen can become toxic leading to uncontrolled spasms and consequent drowning. The waste product of breathing is carbon dioxide. This too is a poisonous gas at pressure of depth. Bob Raimo was enduring at least two of these hazards during this dive. Air is thought not to be a suitable gas for breathing during deep diving.

ON YOUR MARKS IN THE
RACE FOR DEPTH

When it comes to breaking records, rivalry can be intense, but it's entertaining for those of us on the sidelines.

"Controversy surrounded the record-breaking wreck dive attempt off the Channel Islands by UK diver Mark Andrews and his French colleague Jerome Meynie," reported Chris Stone of BBC Radio Jersey.

"The Jersey-based diver who had arranged to video the attempt, Mark Ellyatt, dropped down to the wreck before the others. When they failed to arrive he completed the dive solo – leaving Andrews most unhappy."

Andrews and his associates had spent months preparing for the 170 m (558 ft) dive on a wreck believed to be the *Baden*, a World War I German battleship, sunk as a result of gunnery practice by the Allies after hostilities ended. The wreck lies upside down in Hurd Deep off Alderney.

With the intention to spend 25 minutes exploring the wreck followed by a nine-hour ascent to take into account the required decompression stops, Mark Andrews had claimed he had raised around £100 000 in sponsorship to pay for the costs. This included a backup team of 20 divers and helpers, 34 gas cylinders, compressor, booster pump, the charter of the dive boat *Wey Chieftain*, a support vessel and two large inflatables.

Storms delayed his departure from Portland so he arrived only on the day of the dive, 25th July 2000. It was the day that Concorde crashed in Paris. Mark Andrews had originally intended to be based in Alderney and carry out warm-up dives before the attempt.

Another Mark, Mark Ellyatt, arrived from Jersey where he lived, with two RIBs and three support divers and carried out the dive, citing as evidence his dive computers, which showed a maximum depth of 167.1 m (523 ft), plus the material recorded by his video camera.

Ellyatt said he rendezvoused with the record-seekers' flotilla of boats above the wreck at about 3.30pm, to be ready for slack water at around 5.00pm. His own plan involved a more modest 14-minute bottom time. He had dived several times before in the area, including a 180 m (585 ft) bounce dive – a dive made with only a short pause at the bottom. Hurd Deep is well known among locals for its strong tidal flow.

Ellyatt said he was ready at the right time, but noticed that the main team was having problems deploying their shot-line accurately. What happened next was farcical.

The record-seeking divers, Andrews and Meynie, might have practised endlessly back home for this event, but loaded with an unusual number of gas tanks required to carry out their plan, they found they had no exit point by which they could leave their boat. It was the one detail they had not considered. The doorway was too narrow. They managed to get jammed in the tail-lift of the boat. The pair wore quad bottles and side-mounts.

Unaware of any of this, Mark Ellyatt had already entered the water at the moment the tide slackened and with his video camera at the ready, descended on his own shot-line to prepare for the dive at 6 m (20 ft). He claimed that this was after signalling to Mark Andrews' boat. He then continued on down to the wreck and waited there for them.

Meanwhile, tempers had flared on *Wey Chieftain*. They also found that their hat-mounted lights were fitted with cables to the battery packs that were too short, which restricted their head movements. When they finally got into the water, the tide had started to run. Mark Andrews got down to little more than 7 m (23 ft) deep while the other record-attempt diver is said to have made it to 14 m (45 ft).

When Andrews and Meynie failed to appear, Ellyatt was slightly confused as to why. He assumed that somehow he had missed them and they were still on the wreck but out of sight. He prepared to ascend.

After a few moments getting tangled with his own shot-line, which had become taught thanks to the action of an increasing tidal flow, he completed the dive as planned. He ascended at a safe rate, receiving decompression tanks to breathe from that were handed to him by two of his faithful support divers, but found he had drifted around eight miles from where the group had started in the rapidly accelerating current. By then *Wey Chieftain* and its support boats had left the area was nowhere to be seen.

It appears that while the two record seekers had been floundering at the surface, Mark Ellyatt had inadvertently made a record-breaking dive. Meanwhile, the others had set off for home in disgust.

Ellyatt gives a full account of his dive in his book *Ocean Gladiator*. He told later that he breathed trimix 20/30 down to 60 m (195 ft), then switched to a bottom mix from there down and back to 66 m (215 ft) of which 8 per cent was oxygen, 67 per cent helium and 25 per cent nitrogen.

He switched back to trimix 20/30 up to 21 m (68 ft), then nitrox mixes of 55 per cent to 9 m (30 ft) and 80 per cent to the surface.

"Conditions weren't ideal, but there was some colourful life and not too much current," Mark Ellyatt remembered later. He had been unimpressed by the other team's failure to complete the dive.

"The more I practise, the luckier I get," he said quoting the golfer Arnold Palmer. "If you want to dive in Channel Island waters, then that's where you have to do your training and preparation," he claimed. "I spoke with Mark Andrews several times beforehand about the tides and conditions, but he seemed to have got them confused."

"I'm pleased to have made the dive and set a new record, although I didn't do it for the glory. I just expected to be an unpaid cameraman for the other two."

Meanwhile Mark Andrews was furious. He claimed, "Mark Ellyatt used an unsafe shot-line that did not belong to him, and descended without telling anyone."

He also claimed that Ellyatt had to borrow decompression gas from him to complete his dive, although Ellyatt argues this was only a single tank of air picked up from *Wey Chieftain* at the last moment so that his team would not have to wear a twinset down to the 9 m (30 ft) stop.

Andrews admitted, however, that he had miscalculated the tides, and had trouble getting into the water to anchor the dive platform to the shot-line in time to hit slack water.

Once down at only 6 m (20 ft) deep, Andrews found conditions too dangerous and chose to abort the dive. After training for the dive almost continuously all year, the team suffered massive disappointment and many were said to be visibly trembling with adrenalin aftershock. The *Wey Chieftain* had departed for Portland before Ellyatt surfaced.

Andrews said he was unhappy about the way things worked out, and discounted Ellyatt's having broken a wreck-diving record "because of the way it was done". He criticised him for diving solo in unsafe conditions and without what he saw as sufficient backup.

"Mark was ill-prepared for the dive and had little if any support," he claimed. "I see him as nothing more than a danger to himself and others. If we had not been there he would have had to surface short of his required decompression. I won't be beaten. I'll be back in September with my team and sponsors behind me to do it right."

Ellyatt said he found the criticism he had received surprising. He later said, "I'm only guilty of being prepared."

He said he received plenty of congratulatory phone calls and e-mails from those who heard about the record along with some less than complimentary ones from the record-attempt team who accused him of hijacking their project and calling him among other things an ocean terrorist! Mark Andrews has yet to return to attempt the dive. Mark Ellyatt returned to the wreck one year later.

DAVE SHAW'S VERY DEEP CAVE DIVE

A world record-breaking deep cave dive ends in the recovery of not one but two bodies.

People find different reasons to go diving. For some it is the interaction with the marine animals. For others it's the lure of possible treasure. Some are happy to visit the rusting hulks that once were magnificent vessels. Others are dedicated underwater cave explorers. For some it is the depth, the feeling of getting to somewhere that no man has been to before.

Dave Shaw, an Australian airline pilot living in Hong Kong and working as a training captain for Cathay Pacific, was introduced to diving by his son. He immediately knew that technical diving, with the use of special equipment and complex breathing-gas mixes, was his area of interest. Once he had completed a cave diving course, he was hooked.

He always claimed that depth was of secondary importance to him. His primary interest was exploring. To be where no other man had been before was his ultimate aim, and to achieve that goal, greater depths had become a must.

His pursuit of dives to greater depths led him to seek out Don Shirley, an Englishman based in South Africa. Shirley taught deep diving in a flooded mine at Komati Springs. The two became friends and Shaw sought to dive in the infamous Boesmansgat Cave (Bushman's Hole) where renowned cave diver Nuno Gomes had previously set a record for deep cave diving, and where Shirley had already mounted several expeditions.

It's a vast bell-shaped cave without any natural light. Diving it means descending a line in what is otherwise an environment black as pitch. The line makes the only visual reference. The diver has to deal with the sense of sensory deprivation in addition to the pressures incurred by depth.

In October 2004, equipped with a specially modified closed-circuit rebreather, Dave Shaw dropped to the base of the cave in a successful attempt at the world record for the deepest dive on a closed-circuit rebreather, the greatest depth in a cave on a rebreather, the greatest depth while commencing a dive at altitude and the greatest depth running a line. Shaw's dive was an astonishing 270 m (878 ft) deep. More significantly in the process, he discovered the remains of a diver.

It turned out to be the body of Deon Dreyer, who had lost his life ten years previously when training in order to be a support diver to Nuno Gomes when he achieved his deep cave diving record.

Shaw attempted to lift the body but it was firmly stuck in the mud, so he tied a line to it to make it easy to find another time in the darkness. From then on it became a mission, almost a religious mission, to recover the body of Deon Dreyer and big plans were made.

At this point Dave had completed a little over 300 dives but he was confident about the technicalities. Bret Gilliam, a deep diver with many thousands of hours under water, warned that there was a lot of difference between visiting the depths for a moment and working there.

Dave was not to be put off. Don Shirley gathered together a group of support divers and helped him cover the intricate logistics. Dave wrote on his website, "The dive will be unique and huge. I plan on spending up to five minutes at 270 m (878 ft) recovering the body. That will equate to a 680-minute dive on CCR. If I have to bail out the dive will extend to 764 minutes. The bailout gas will involve

19×11.4 l (80 cu. ft) tanks, using seven different mixes. If all goes to plan I will still be flushing on to the seven different mixes during the ascent. The deepest bailout tanks will be at 150 m (480 ft). I will carry 4 × 11.4 l (80 cu. ft) tanks with me so as to have sufficient gas to get from 270 m (886 ft) to 150 m (492 ft). At the bottom, one tank will last just 3–4 minutes . . . as you can see, the planning task is significant."

It was only two months before they had all the equipment, and personnel in place to attempt the recovery of the body. David Shaw died during this deep dive on 8th January 2005.

Shaw was equipped at the time with an underwater camera and its recording gave valuable information that allowed others to determine that he suffered from "an effort-independent expiratory flow which resulted in an inability to match ventilation to the demands of physical work at that great depth".

In simple terms, the demands of his heavy breathing could not be matched by the supply from his breathing equipment nor, the ability of the chemical scrubber of the rebreather to eliminate the poisonous carbon dioxide he exhaled.

A body bag was thought to be the only option for Dreyer's body, as all the professional advice given was that the body would be just a skeleton held together by a wet suit. It might have fallen apart on ascent. On the October dive, the body was stuck in the mud held by the cylinders, and the plan was to cut it loose, after the legs were placed in the bag. Shaw had run into problems when Dreyer's body unexpectedly became difficult to handle as it floated up out of the mud. Enclosed within its wetsuit, Dreyer's mortal remains had turned into a soap-like substance. It had become "adipocerous", which evidently made it almost neutrally buoyant.

The powerful underwater lights that cave divers use are connected by waterproof cable to battery canisters that are normally worn on the cave diver's waist, or sometimes attached to their BC (buoyancy control device) or tanks. Working with both hands, Shaw had resorted to resting the head of his canister light on the cave floor. The cave line that had been laid to the body the previous October, got tangled in the light head and quickly cocooned both Shaw and the corpse while he was attempting to get Dreyer's body into the bag. The physical effort of trying to free himself led to Shaw's death.

Don Shirley had been his deepest support diver. He survived a dive to 250 m (812 ft) but not without suffering severe decompression illness caused during the ascent and a dramatic rescue. The electronic handset of the rebreather he was using had imploded at depth due to the extreme pressure.

Because of the entanglement with the lines, a week later the bodies of both Shaw and Dreyer floated up to near the surface. This happened as the dive support team was pulling up those lines to recover their own equipment that included deco gas cylinders. Dave's light head was tangled in the October dive's cave line, which now cocooned the body of Dreyer and which was suspended below Shaw. They were recovered.

The dive on which David Shaw died was the 333rd of his career. At the time of his world record-setting dive, he had been diving for just over five years.

PART FOUR

Famous Wrecks and Other Adventures

AIRACOBRA IN HANSA BAY

Searching for the wreck of a single-seater plane under water can be both frustrating and disappointing until local help is enlisted.

"Go! Go! Go!" William's instructions were clear as he tumbled head first from the aft deck of the boat and finned down as hard as he could, pulling at the same time on the rear dump of his BC to be sure no trapped air was impeding his descent.

He reached the seabed at 30 m (98 ft) in less than a minute but there was nothing to see, just sand. Acres and acres of it, stretching in seductive humps as far as the eye could see, which was only about 15 m (50 ft). But wait, there was a dark patch. He headed towards it, but there was nothing. Another dark patch, there was nothing there either. After chasing more of these shadows, he began to realise that the dark patches were caused by either light refraction or the mind tricks of sensory deprivation, looking for something where there was nothing.

He headed carefully back to the surface and eventually climbed wearily back on to the dive platform of the boat. Others had just done similar fruitless exercises, chasing down to investigate what might have made the raised contour line revealed on the vessel's echo-sounder.

They were looking for the wreck of a small fighter plane, a Bell Aira-cobra P-39, that ditched in the sea during an attack on Japanese supply ships in Hansa Bay, Papua New Guinea, in 1943 during World War II.

The problem was that the fuselage of such a small wreck stood less than a metre clear of the seabed and it was hard to distinguish it on the echo-sounder from what were simply humps of sand.

After another couple of hours of painstaking search with the boat doing tight grid patterns and everyone staring blankly at the level trace on the sounder, it was time to ask for help.

Life in Papua New Guinea has remained mainly unchanged over the centuries for the locals. They still live in the tribal long houses in their villages, go fishing from canoes dug out from the trunks of trees and many still wear local attire.

The divers approached a lonely outrigger canoe complete with fisherman who was totally naked apart from a traditional decorative penis sheath. Unsteadily inside its fragile hull sat the man and his baby son. Tony Collins, their captain, shouted to him in pidgin, the only word of which they grasped was "Youbla!"

He then continued to ask the question. The fisherman nodded back positively and started to paddle furiously as they meandered along behind him in *Moonlighting*, their Grand Banks motor yacht. It must have made a very strange sight indeed! Modern seafarers have come to rely on all manner of electronic aids like GPS and digital echo-sounders. Those brought up in more primitive societies develop a feeling for their environment that to us may be inexplicable.

There, like witchcraft, in the middle of the open ocean, without a transit or landmark in sight that anyone could distinguish, the local man pointed nonchalantly down into the water to where he positively insisted the wrecked plane sat. He simply knew where it was.

They dropped a weighted line topped with a marker buoy and a moment later Tony tossed himself over the side. No one else relished another fruitless search in the deep, over the same old sand. Five minutes later he surfaced.

"She'd be 'right!" he nodded as he slung his aqualung back on to the rack. "I can understand how we could have easily missed the bugger! It's tiny."

The old wing commander, one of the passenger divers, was into his dive kit and off the back of the boat in a trice. He had beaten all of them all week, at getting to the front of the queue. The others headed down to the plane to find him hovering over the fuselage. The drop-weight from the buoy had landed about a metre from it. So much for electronics versus local knowledge!

The Airacobra sat squarely on the seabed. A single-seater aircraft, it looked rather small but the 37 mm cannon in its nose, with its barrel protruding through the propeller boss, was not. They took in the image but something seemed unusual. The great Allinson V engine was in the back, behind the pilot's seat; the prop shaft passed between the pilot's legs. Not a very comfortable-looking option. The wing commander, ever the aviation expert, had immediately spotted why it had crashed. Its tailplane and rudder were missing!

With a wingspan of merely 10 m (33 ft), this was a tiny haven of safety in the eternal abyss for the reef fish that lived in and around it. But it was not entirely safe. The divers soon spotted the most enormous and well-fed lionfish that obviously gorged on the smaller prey it found there.

It was a wonder how these animals had found this place. There seemed to be the whole gamut of Indo-Pacific reef life, including a grouper and two red emperors.

The Japanese were defeated in the battles for the Kokoda Trail because their supply lines were destroyed. Although they had built numerous airstrips and improvised harbours along the coast of New Guinea, their naval losses at the Battle of Guadalcanal in the Solomons and their defeat in the Battle of the Coral Sea had put them at a severe disadvantage.

An allied coast-watcher identified transports unloading supplies in Hansa Bay, around 200 km (124 miles) from Madang on the Bismark Sea coast. For the American Air Force the attack had been something less of a battle and more of a turkey-shoot. It has been recorded that 34 wrecked vessels now lie, mostly undiscovered and undived, in the bay. The ones they had looked at in previous days had been almost bombed to oblivion. The pilot of the USAAF Bell Airacobra must have been really unlucky to be one of the few American losses.

A BRITISH
DESTROYER SUNK

Was this a secret warship wreck in the Red Sea that few else had dived?

As they approached the wreck site from the open sea, they could see in the distance what they thought was a small motor vessel with its rusting bows sticking out of the water. Once they drew closer they realised the scale of things more accurately. It was the sharp end of a warship, and what they had thought initially to be superstructure turned out to be the two forward gun turrets. It was hard to believe that this wreck had been totally overlooked by the Egyptian tourist diving industry.

Passing the long promontory of land that forms Ras Banus, the vessel had turned west towards Port Berenice. It was a long way to travel from the scruffy jetty at Hamata, but they sped along at around 16 knots so they were where they needed to be the following morning.

The information as to exactly where the wreck lay, had been kept secret and the visitors had been given strict instructions not to photograph any part of the shoreline that lay nearby. Ahmed Fadel, senior dive-guide with Emperor Divers, operators of the motor yacht *Elite*, had dived this wreck already but it seemed few either knew of it or could be bothered to make the long trip southwards from Port Galib or Hamata to get to it.

Steve Carmichael-Timson, a former naval man and wreck hunter and one of the passengers, was similarly sworn to secrecy. He had travelled from Britain with a computer-driven side-scan sonar and an underwater metal detector. Neither was needed to find this wreck.

At first glance he thought it looked very much like a British "Zulu Class" destroyer of World War II vintage. It took him no time at all, once back in Britain, to research the vessel and come up with its real identity.

It was HMS *Myngs* R06, a former Royal Navy sub-hunter destroyer built by Vickers Armstrong in Newcastle-upon-Tyne and launched in 1943. It was commissioned in 1944 and its main armaments were its 4.5-inch guns and eight Mk 9 21-inch torpedoes. The vessel had taken part in an action to destroy an enemy convoy off the Norwegian coast in November 1944.

It was one of four similar vessels that became redundant after the war and were sold off at the same time in 1955. HMS *Zenith* and HMS *Myngs* were sold to the Egyptians while HMS *Zealous* and HMS *Zodiac* were each sold to the Israelis. There was a political storm at the time but you can't say the British government wasn't even-handed.

HMS *Myngs* was renamed *El Qaher*. It had been refitted in India and then intended to serve in the Egyptian navy. Its rusting bow section still securely held in place 37 years later reflected the fact that it had been caught at anchor by Israeli single-seater jet fighters on the morning of 16th May 1970, during the interval between the 6-Day and Yom Kippur wars.

It had obviously been the scene of some savage fighting, but eventually the ship had succumbed to the onslaught, sinking on to a ledge on which today, her hull hung precariously, leaving the bows clear of the surface. The whole vessel was now held by its starboard anchor.

If things looked bad at the surface they were far worse under water. Strafing with cannon fire and exploding aerial bombs had devastated the vessel. The command centre had been blown to smithereens. The gun turrets looked as though they had been a hive of activity during the desperate attempt to save the vessel but to no avail. The 40 mm Bofors anti-aircraft gun emplacement had taken a direct hit, but not before it had strewn the seabed nearby with spent cartridge cases that must have sizzled as they hit the water. The torpedo launchers were empty but not deployed. The whole vessel was now encased in soft corals and had become a haven for thousands of fishes.

As the divers descended through plankton-loaded water, oversized Bohar snappers dispersed in the gloom ahead of them. A giant grouper or true wreck-fish hung around under the hull where it overhung the reef ledge. The divers could never get close enough to photograph it. Reticence is what allows a fish like that to live so long and achieve such gargantuan dimensions.

Grandad-size sweetlips and a solitary super-male Napoleon wrasse hung around there too. A giant puffer fish lolled around on top of an aft gun turret, unperturbed or just too lazy to move when it had a big camera thrust up to its face. It was still in the same place several hours later.

The propellers now at a depth of around 21 m (68 ft) could give anyone a serious case of propeller envy. They were enormous and obviously designed to be sufficient to hurtle the vessel along at a huge rate of knots. Today, they are covered in soft corals and sponges that lit up in vibrant shades of scarlet and pink in the beam of a lamp. The seabed alongside the wreck was a complete turmoil of displaced equipment and spent shell cases. Jacks hunted among the chaos of what was the stricken warship while the surface around the forward area was a solid shining mass of silversides so dense, the divers couldn't see the surface past them.

They scraped the "mung" off a few plates to reveal the original English inscriptions. A 4.5-inch shell lay ready to fire in the breach of the gun at the aft, destined never to fulfil its intended role before it found its watery resting place.

The divers were able to examine closely what remained of the forward-facing sonar installation that was revealed in the lifted part of the hull forward. Its dome had been blown off with the force of some explosion and lay on the seabed beneath it, and was now the home to some cute juvenile bannerfish.

Not cute at all, a toothy giant barracuda the size of a small shark hung menacingly, waiting for them in the shadow under *Elite*, which initially had been tied off to the wreck. It followed them around on their next dive like some aging caretaker making sure they didn't steal anything.

The liveaboard soon had to be moved away from the wreck. An Egyptian naval officer arrived with a boarding party in a small official dinghy. They came from the secret naval base that was clearly visible on the distant shore. There were some tense moments, but after some discussion he compromised, and they conceded to his authority by moving their vessel to a position that allowed them to see the base more clearly and the people in the base to see them more clearly too!

Evidently, they had permission to dive the wreck from the coastguard and the security services, but not from the navy to park their vessel nearby. It meant further dives could be had only after a long ride in the inflatable boats. Thankfully, the sea was flat-calm and it was not too arduous in the mid-summer sun. All the secrecy seemed misplaced later when it was noticed that the wreck was clearly visible on Google Earth[TM].

USS *SARATOGA* CV3

The Japanese didn't manage to sink her during the Pacific War despite several attempts, but she finally succumbed to the effects of an atomic bomb detonated by her own side.

U p to 80 warships were sunk by an atomic bomb at Bikini Atoll in the Pacific Marshall Islands, in a demonstration of tactical nuclear power by the Americans in 1946. The USS *Saratoga* CV3, a very famous vessel, was one of them.

Together with the *Lexington*, she was the USA's first proper aircraft carrier and accommodated up to 90 aircraft. At 271 m (888 ft) long, she was longer than the *Titanic*, had a 32 m (105 ft) beam and weighed in at 33 000 tons. At the time of her sinking, she was one of the biggest aircraft carriers in the world. The Japanese claimed to have sunk her seven times. She saw action throughout World War II in campaigns at Wake Island, Guadalcanal, the Gilbert and Marshall Islands, Sumatra, Java and she was hit by five Kamikaze attacks at Iwo Jima. The *Saratoga* had more than 1000 watertight compartments and although she was moored only 300 m (984 ft) from the "Baker" atomic undersea detonation at Bikini, she still took eight hours to sink. This vessel was armed with twelve 5-inch guns, eight 0.50 mm machine guns, 30 Oerlikon anti-aircraft guns and four quad 40 mm Bofors guns. She now sits upright on the bottom of the lagoon, among the other wrecks, the star of the show.

Dropping through what seems to be an eternal void, not five astronauts floating in space but five aquanauts in an expanse of emptiness, Fabio's twin tanks gleam in the sunshine below the others, but they're in more of a never-ending grey than the deep blue they might have expected. A solitary grey reef shark, complete with remora, climbs slowly up towards them from the deep, curious to know what these noisy creatures are that have entered its domain, and then they see the bottom – but it's not the seabed. Instead it's a bed of regularly planted rivets, neatly positioned in rows that stream off to a visual infinity in each direction. With only 18 m (60 ft) of horizontal visibility you can easily lose your bearings on a deck that is nearly 273 m (896 ft) long by more than 30 m (98 ft) wide. The wooden decking long gone, it's a steel desert big enough to land a plane on, or indeed several.

They reach a landmark, the precipice that drops from the ship's rail to the sandy bottom another 25 m (80 ft) below. They drop over and hover by a group of anti-aircraft guns, mounted on a balcony with a sea view. There's the unmistakable shape of a forklift truck incongruously abandoned, left out overnight and ruined in the atomic rain.

Everything is of Brobdingnagian proportions. There are massive five-inch guns. One, mounted in a turret on the foredeck, is so large it defies any skill to photograph it in the reduced visibility. The anchor hangs from the bow; another is lying way below on the sand. One link of its chain is bigger than the torso of a man and it pours from an enormous maw in the hull, the hawse-pipe strewn with whip coral. They peer down, trying to get a glimpse of what lies below. It's hard to contemplate that there's at least another 25 m (80 ft) between them and the seabed.

It's time to wend their way along the edge of the deck, past the open hatch to a bomb elevator and back to the superstructure. They have to swim more than 100 m (325 ft) from the bow. Their maximum depth has been less than 33 m (107 ft), but computers already show deco-stops with 30 minutes of total ascent time needed.

At 25 m (80 ft) deep they take a peek into the admiral's day room. His bed is still there together with the speaking tubes that kept him in touch with goings-on at the bridge. At 18 m (60 ft) they enter the control centre. It's a fortress with slit windows for outward views. The binnacle is still present as are all the other controls. Fabio indicates a series of giant dials. Next door, the captain's day room waits. A sink, its wooden cabinets long gone, is held up by its plumbing. Outside, a small fly-bridge piled up with several brass portholes, perhaps collected by an earlier visitor and given second thoughts, lies abandoned among a spaghetti of broken cables.

A crowd of batfish obscure the site of their first short stop at 15 m (50 ft) at the topmast. Then it's a short swim to where the trapeze hangs, its regulators dangling on long hoses that feed the nitrox 80 (a gas mix low in nitrogen) to them, for a period passing silly messages on slates. The boredom of waiting here is worth it in exchange for the extraordinary experience below. Finally, it's back to the dive boat and the searing tropical Pacific sunshine.

This is Jim Breakell's first trip here. As a diving holiday operator he intends to come again and bring lots of his clients with him. He later queries with Fabio Amaral, the Brazilian diver who's made diving here possible, that many British divers would query the use of air for dives at this depth. Many modern divers would only think of using a trimix, a gas mix of oxygen, nitrogen and helium, for this sort of diving. It's not possible to fly helium into Bikini Atoll. Oxygen is generated on site.

Fabio is an impressive-looking man, 2 metres tall and built like a battleship. He doesn't suffer fools gladly. He doesn't have to. Fabio looks Jim straight in the eye.

"Tell them we don't want them here," he growls.

An aircraft carrier is as big as an airfield. It has to be. The *Saratoga* was once the biggest aircraft carrier in the American fleet, a military leviathan, a city on the sea. It's a massive machine of war. No diver can see much of it during the time limitations of a single dive.

Next, they visit a hangar deck. The floor is knee-deep in rust particles. One ill-judged fin kick can turn the water to Brown Windsor soup. Their lamps reveal aero-engines and plane propellers. Rows of bombs are lined up ready to be loaded and Helldivers still sit waiting to be catapulted into the sky. It's a dark and gloomy place. They're glad to find a way out into the eternal space of the daylight.

If the *Saratoga* were the only wreck in the lagoon it would be worth the trip. But it isn't. The seabed at Bikini Atoll is crowded with World War II warships, and the *Saratoga* is only one of many sunk in that post-war demonstration of atomic power. Only a few privileged divers have ever been able to visit them.

DIVING THE *TITANIC*

Of all shipwrecks, the *Titanic* must be the most iconic, but it's far beyond the range of ordinary scuba divers.

O wner of a successful, air-conditioning company, Carl Spencer was a keen amateur diver who made it his business to dive with the best technical wreck divers Britain had to offer. When he got the chance to visit the *Titanic* in a MIR deep-water submarine in 2003, he jumped at it and invited his friend Kevin Gurr to go with him.

The main purpose of the dive was to clean up some of the paraphernalia left behind after a Discovery Channel filming expedition led by director James Cameron, with whom Carl was a friend.

"I could barely contain my excitement at the thought of diving the MIR. A few years ago this technology would not have been available to the West, let alone a plumber from Dudley!" he wrote in his Internet diary. "Genya is considered the best submersible pilot in Russia and his skills later in the dive proved it. The hatch was secured and we were ready for launch. The first thing that struck me was the silence. We could see the activity aboard *Keldysh* (the mother ship) during the launch, but there was absolutely no sound at all."

They left the surface in MIR 2 at 10.00am in the morning. Kevin Gurr reminisced later how, during the descent, they talked about the enormous pressures inflicted on the outside of the hull of the little submarine and how failure of the materials would lead to an instant flood and their certain deaths. At that moment, Genya invited him to take the controls.

Kevin sat proudly wishing all his friends could see him at that moment when, without warning, he felt the ominous sensation of water falling on him. He nearly leapt out of his skin.

It seems that a large amount of condensation from the breath of the submarine's occupants regularly collected in the upper part of the cramped cabin and at about this point in the descent it was known to form a large drip that fell on to the pilot. The Russian pilots knew this and felt it was a jolly joke to let a chosen passenger enjoy a sudden fright. The submarine was not leaking.

Two-and-a-half hours later they reached the seabed 3810 m (12 500 ft) deep. That's two-and-a-half miles from the surface. The water outside was minus 2°C (6°F). They sighted the bow of the great ship.

"It absolutely took my breath away, it was huge," continued Carl in his diary. "Now I know what the *Britannic* divers have been raving about all these years (*Britannic* was a sister ship of the *Titanic*). *Titanic* towered above us, even though the bow had ploughed almost 18 m (60 ft) into the seabed. The scale of the ship, anchor chains and so on, was enormous. We worked our way around the bow checking for any possible signs of 'man-made' intrusion or damage, although we saw none. Genya immediately spotted the mast had fallen onto the decks at a heavy angle due to bacterial decay over the last 90 years."

They deployed some experiments on behalf of two scientists and continued around the bow. They looked at the quarters of Captain Smith behind the bridge.

"The telemotor stands alone on the bridge surrounded by plaques laid by previous US, French, Canadian and Russian expeditions. They seem to have lost their significance now there are so many 'dedications to lost souls'. The remaining time on the bow was spent removing fibre-optic cables from the 2001 'Ghosts' expedition. By the end of our time on the bow, we'd removed over 300 m (984 ft) of fibre-optic from Earthship's ROVs – Jake & Elwood."

Personally, they wanted to examine the reciprocating engines. At nearly a 1000 metric tonnes each, they proved bigger than either of them could have imagined. There was also Cameron's fibre-optic cabling to remove here. The two used much of their time theorising how they could tackle an exploration of similar engines on the *Britannic*, for this was their intention, to scuba dive the 120 m (390 ft) deep wreck of the *Titanic*'s sister ship in the Aegean.

The MIR 2 left the bottom at around 7.00 pm. During the ascent they talked about the dive and the condition of the wreck. It gave them time for something to eat. They were quite hungry because they hadn't eaten for 11 hours. Twelve hours after they first submerged they broke the surface.

Kevin Gurr confirmed in an interview with Mark Caney of PADI that the second best dive of his life, although not strictly a technical dive, was a ride in the MIR submersible to the *Titanic* with his friend Carl Spencer. His best dive was his first dive to the *Britannic*.

Sadly, Carl Spencer was killed during a later diving expedition to the *Britannic*. He was part of a 17-strong team commissioned by National Geographic to survey and film both outside and inside the wreck. It was 2009. He was 39 years old.

DON PEDRO

Out of sight and out of mind to tourists who visit a popular Mediterranean island, an enormous wreck is slumbering not too far from the beach.

Millions of Europeans take holidays in Spain's Balearic Islands each year, and the sight of the fleet of modern ships and ferries connecting them to the mainland is familiar to anyone who glances up from a sun bed to view the horizon.

As Spain has become richer, these vessels have become bigger and more sophisticated. Some are as big as office blocks and seem as secure as any of the rocky headlands they pass. One would think it inconceivable that any one of them might be steered into a well-marked reef, but this is exactly what happened on the evening of 11th July 2007.

It was a calm, clear summer's night, and most young tourists in Ibiza Town were noisily partying the night away when the Iscomar Lines roll-on/roll-off container ship and truck ferry, *Don Pedro*, slipped her moorings and left port.

She was a modern vessel, built in 1982 and equipped with every navigation aid available, but she was just reaching her full speed of 12 knots, when her helmsman took a wrong route and piled into a well-marked reef, clearly in sight of their departure point.

The *Don Pedro* was fatally holed, with a 7 m (23 ft) gash along her portside bilge keel. Her 18 crew and two passengers took to the rescue boats. The giant vessel sank from sight within 45 minutes, and now lies on the seabed at around 45 m (146 ft) deep.

The 150 tonnes of heavy fuel oil from *Don Pedro*'s bunkers, along with 50 tonnes of light diesel and containers full of chemicals, including one of old car batteries, threatened to pollute Ibiza's popular beaches and destroy the island's holiday industry.

A long-planned emergency response procedure was put into action. Salvage vessels with divers and all the paraphernalia necessary to halt the oil leaks arrived within a few days.

There followed a careful and well-documented operation to remove the bunker oil and clean those beaches immediately affected. It was not a quick process. Holes had to be cut in the sides of the hull, with a hot-tap system to allow valves to be connected, and the first oil was not pumped out until 30th July. It was a tense time for the residents and businesses of Ibiza, and typical Mediterranean summer storms did little to help. However, the operation was triumphant and no further damage to the island's tourism business was done.

In the year that passed following the wrecking, arguments raged as to whether to raise *Don Pedro* or leave the wreckage where it was. It formed no hazard to shipping, and at the start of July 2008 the authorities unexpectedly announced that it would be open to leisure divers, though internal penetration of it was forbidden for reasons of safety. At 142 m (461 ft) long, this ferry is now one of the Mediterranean's bigger and more easily accessible wrecks.

One of the first to dive it was an Italian-Cockney from London, Diego Leonardi. He was a disturbingly pretty young man with such gorgeously luxuriant hair, that he preferred to stick his mask on his face without a strap to tangle, allowing water pressure alone to keep it in place. He worked as an instructor at a nearby dive centre.

He and his photographer buddy dropped through the gloom to find this office block of a wreck lying forlornly on its side. They made straight for the propeller. This would be the deepest part of their dive, at around 40 m (130 ft), and the photographer wanted to get a shot of Diego dwarfed by the enormous fan that formerly drove the ship along. Ever the underwater poseur, Diego was happy to oblige.

It was pretty chilly down there too, despite it being midsummer. They saw only 16°C (60°F) recorded on their computers, and reflected that they were glad to be wearing drysuits with plenty of thermal underwear. They made their way round the stern, past the massive rear doors that previously doubled as an access ramp and up onto the stairway that had been built to lead to different levels of the superstructure. Rope work that had formerly been in place had fallen away. Deck paraphernalia had fallen over onto the walls. Steel ships that lose their ability to float hit the seabed with a significant clout, resulting in chaos of anything not strong enough to take the thudding deceleration.

Already the wreck had been adopted by some wildlife. Huge Mediterranean scorpion fish lay everywhere, bright orange in colour and were reluctant to move even when confronted by these startling air-bubbling visitors.

The divers passed around the superstructure at the aft end of the wreck, checking out the radar towers and wheelhouse, and made the long swim to the bow, dramatic with its bulbous leading keel, massive winches and huge anchors still in place.

The occasional conger eel popped its head out from where it was hiding to see who was disturbing its rest, and ubiquitous Mediterranean brown combers hung around aimlessly. On the way, Diego stopped to clean some of the mung off the hull to reveal the ship's name painted along its side, but he was reminded that they needed to keep their dive, and hence their decompression time, short.

Safely back on board their dive boat, they were soon being flung at around 30 knots through a less than kind sea, passing another "office block" but one that was under way. It was the *Don Fernando*, sister ship of the ill-fated *Don Pedro*, leaving port. They weren't the first to see around the submerged wreck, but they were among the first leisure divers. It gave a certain satisfaction to know what lay unseen but so close to the busy beaches.

THE *DUNRAVEN*
AND T. E. LAWRENCE

Never let the truth get in the way of a good story.

As a young man, American Israeli Howard Rosenstein, with his big black beard, evoked a fearless image. During the early days of the development of the sport of diving, it was his faith in the potential of the Red Sea, that kick-started an industry. He created the *Dunraven* story before he ever knew the wreck existed.

In the mid-1970s the Sinai was occupied by Israel. Howard was struggling to keep his rather basic Red Sea Divers centre at Na'ama Bay afloat because visiting divers were few and far between. The devastating effects of the Yom Kippur War of 1973 were still being felt, and his dive centre was in serious threat of closing down.

The movie, *The Deep*, was a big box office hit at the time. It extolled the adventure and mystery of sunken wrecks and treasure, and had done a lot to promote diving tourism to the Caribbean. One of the divers working at the Red Sea Divers centre came up with the bright idea of discovering their very own sunken treasure ship!

It was a great idea with only one flaw. In the five years that they had been in operation, they had yet to find one shipwreck in the waters off the Sinai. Ever resourceful, Howard made up a fantastic story about Lawrence of Arabia, gold payments to the Bedouin fighters, and of course, the rumour that one of the ships went down close by.

Armed with a plausible story, they were desperate to find at least one sunken ship that could fit the bill and be masqueraded as that treasure ship. In the meantime they subtly planted the story with the journalists who were coming to their Red Sea outpost to cover the new phenomenon of Red Sea diving tourism.

Of course, they told each one of them that they would be the first to get the "scoop" once they decided to make the location of the ship public, but for the time being, they were keeping its location secret for "obvious reasons".

Luckily for them and their diminishing credibility, rumours started reaching the environs of Sharm el Sheikh that some fishermen had found what they believed to be a shipwreck. They thought they could see its silhouette from the surface and they were catching many large fish in its vicinity.

A Bedouin fisherman named Suleiman was the source of these stories. Howard and his crew were off to see him to try to get its position. Suleiman was amicable and shared the position as much as he knew it.

"Go to Ras Mohammed, turn the corner heading west into the Suez and after two cigarettes, you will see waves breaking on an off-shore reef. Go to the far south-western corner and that is where the ship can be found."

In his words, Howard "made a big deal of a shipwreck expedition" and convinced Carl Roessler, an American pioneer of dive travel in those days, to join him with a group of intrepid American diving tourists.

At the first opportunity they loaded up their rusting "Metal Boat". It was a 14 m (45 ft) long, converted coastal patrol boat, which had lived nearly all its life in the Sea of Galilee and had only recently been purchased by Red Sea Divers. It was not ideal for the purpose.

Following Suleiman's less than precise directions and taking to smoking cigarettes instead of his trusty pipe, Howard and his party headed around Ras Mohammed at the southernmost point of the Sinai and into the Gulf of Suez. Sure enough, two cigarettes later, they were heading towards what appeared to be breaking waves where there was nothing indicated on the maritime chart of the area. They found the tip of what is now known to be Sha'ab Mahmoud reef, or "Beacon Rock".

From here it was anyone's guess where the wreck was to be found. Howard instructed his skipper to take the dive boat to the most western point of the reef and gear up for a dive. He wasn't expecting too much. However, as soon as he hit the water and the moment the bubbles from his impact had dissipated, right below his feet was the distinct outline of a ship. It was covered in corals and lying about 15 m (50 ft) below him.

The excitement of discovery for all aboard was beyond description. Everyone rushed to gear up and within minutes ten adventurous tourists were diving this historic wreck to which Howard immediately attached the "Lawrence of Arabia treasure ship" saga. It was too good a story to miss.

Needless to say, once the word got out, everyone else in Sharm el Sheikh claimed they already knew of the wreck and half the people in the fledging diving business there, also claimed to have been the first to find it. If the truth were told, nobody will ever know who the first was and it doesn't really matter. The fact is Howard Rosenstein finally had his wreck and now it was time to get down to business, using this discovery for the benefit of diving tourism in Sharm.

Over the next year, he and his divers continued to dive and explore the wreck, which was very attractive and exciting for all of them. On one of the very first trips, the then American Ambassador, Samuel Lewis, joined them and they encountered the very first identifying artefacts on the ship; plates and cups which clearly had the name "Dunraven" glazed on them.

At the time, no one had a clue as to the true identity of the *Dunraven*, but the Lawrence of Arabia saga lived on, and in fact had become pretty much established in the professional diving circles of the day.

Jack McKinney, editor of the American diving magazine, *Skin Diver*, indicated a desire to come out to the Sinai to write a feature about the Lawrence of Arabia wreck, and even better, to make a film about it. This was a dream come true for Howard, a man desperate for some publicity to generate more business.

The big day came and Jack and his glamorous wife and model Sari, disembarked with a ton of gear in Sharm and started his coverage of diving and of course, the newly discovered treasure ship. Subsequently, a cover story of this trip in *Skin Diver* magazine and a very popular diving film *God's Other World – the Red Sea*, sang the praises of the special quality of Red Sea diving. The Lawrence of Arabia treasure ship was the pivotal sequence in the production and Howard's plans of putting the Red Sea on to the international diving tourism map were finally taking off. The ball was starting to roll.

When the producers of the BBC's prestigious documentary program *The World About Us* indicated their interest in filming the wreck because of the attention it was attracting, Howard instantly agreed. The people at Red Sea Divers quickly learned though that the BBC has its own way of doing things and they weren't buying everything they were being sold about Lawrence of Arabia. The BBC had a whole team researching this wreck and it was only through their efforts, that the real identity of the *Dunraven* was unravelled, together with its secrets including its sinking in 1876, long before the Great War.

No gold was ever found but a treasure of stories, adventures and amazing people have shared the *Dunraven* saga. The northern Red Sea's first shipwreck available to divers, became a keystone in the burgeoning Red Sea diving tourism appeal.

Ambassador Lewis was later to play an important role in the Camp David Peace treaty, which allowed for the return of the Sinai to Egypt. He was a very enthusiastic diver and perhaps did as much as anyone to secure the continuation of diving tourism in Egypt after the Israeli withdrawal in 1982.

GALLIPOLI WARS

It promised to be a fantastic trip to dive the sunken Dreadnoughts of Gallipoli, but it proved to be another disaster.

The World War I campaign to force a passage through Turkey's Dardanelles was intended to enable the Allies to bolster Russia in its fight against Germany. Since Russia was the traditional enemy of the Turks, that country had allied itself to Germany, although had things been different, it might equally well have allied itself to Britain and France.

There followed an ill-conceived action on behalf of the Royal Navy. Although the naval guns outranged the Turkish land batteries at the narrows of Çanakkale, its mighty fleet of 63 Dreadnought-class battle-ships, so named for their supposed invulnerability, supported by 180 other vessels, proved no match for the actions of a solitary little Turkish minelayer, the *Nusrat*.

The HMS *Ocean*, the HMS *Irresistible* and the French battleship *Bouvet* together with five other cruisers were sunk within a few hours. The strong currents and geographical bottleneck of the Dardanelles also set up the British and French vessels for easy attack by German U-boats.

It was equally ill-conceived when an expeditionary land-force of British, ANZAC and other Empire soldiers, under General Ian

Hamilton, was then sent to capture the Gallipoli peninsula in the face of its Turkish defenders.

The ill-placed confidence of the British invaders was evident by the fact that on landing at Suvla Bay they stopped for tea and a game of cricket. This gave the Turkish army with its German advisers, time to organise and take the high ground from the few New Zealanders who were unlucky enough to have been sent to defend it. Without that crucial four-hour delay the outcome might have been entirely different.

Fighting local soldiers who were defending their homes and with nowhere to retreat, gave British commanders their first taste of what the United States was to experience later in Vietnam. A total of 250 000 men were lost on each side at a rate of 1000 each day. A campaign, which was expected to last only 11 days, took eight months before the inevitable retreat. It was a military disaster.

Winston Churchill, then First Lord of the Admiralty, reported that the ghosts of Gallipoli were to haunt him for the rest of his life.

When the Royal Navy was seen to retreat to the safety of the open sea, the morale of the land forces was severely damaged. The HMS *Majestic*, one of the oldest Dreadnoughts in the fleet, was sent back to patrol the coast as a sacrifice to political expediency. A German U-boat operating at Cape Hellas soon sank her. The Gallipoli campaigns, both naval and land based, were ill-considered and ill-conceived. The idea to market a diving vacation to dive the wrecks of Gallipoli was probably equally ill-conceived.

An expeditionary group composed of three journalists, a freelance radio reporter and a number of fare-paying divers set off with the promise of spending a week on a luxury liveaboard dive boat, the *Artemis*, diving the wrecks of the *Majestic*, HMS *Triumph*, HMS *Irresistible*, HMS *Goliath* and the Turkish battleship *Messudieh*.

It was a seductive idea that was made more promising by the fact that one of their number was a direct descendant of General Ian Hamilton and bore his name. When asked for a quote this good-natured Canadian, with a definite Scottish complexion, betrayed his optimism by suggesting that while his Great Uncle had famously told his soldiers to "Dig, dig, dig!" he thought they should get ready to "Dive, dive, dive!"

During a stop-off in Istanbul at the museum he runs, Selçuk Kolay added to building a sense of expectation by beguiling the group with stories of the deep wrecks that he had dived with the aid of trimix.

Alas, the only major intact wreck they were to see during the week was that of their own so-called luxury liveaboard – only it was still afloat and ostensibly operating as normal. The *Artemis* is 51 m (168 ft) long but had clearly seen better days. There was some damage above the waterline at the stern. This had been "made good" with plastic filler and a sheet of plywood – a somewhat unusual remedy for a repair to a steel hull.

Ever optimistic, the group moved their things on board, trying not to be disconcerted by cabins that were barely bigger than the combined lavatory and shower cubicle they included. In fact they were really lavatories with en-suite sleeping facilities rather than the more usual alternative. The only air-conditioning in evidence was that provided by the occupant's own bowel movements. At night the generator was turned off, which denied anyone accurate use of the windowless cubicle, and there were some tense moments in the morning while they awaited the engineer's listless awakening and the restarting of each individual's bodily functions.

The passengers were given strict instructions to avoid putting any used paper in the lavatories and instead to use the bin provided. There was also the instruction to remove the unused roll before attempting to take a shower.

The shower hose was short so that it was necessary to sit on the toilet to wash – but the water provided was merely a cool and brackish trickle. Some were luckier than others. Those with cabins below decks enjoyed a greater quantity of water from the surrounding sea. It found its way through the perforated hull on to their cabin floor or worse, their beds.

Beds were another issue. The bed linen was filthy and those who found incontrovertible evidence of this beneath their pillows, substantiated the idea that it had not been changed after previous occupants. Neither were sheets changed during their stay. The never-emptied bins in the toilets became unspeakably pungent, too.

One redeeming factor was the food. It was mainly beans for the first three days. Although described by some as of very poor quality and devoid of meat, it must be said that only the most sensitive stomach detected any traces of unhygienic standards in its preparation. Alas, the breakfast was normally feta cheese, jam and bread that was so dry it defied belief.

Some passengers became very vocal, while others made tight-lipped observations regarding their cabins and swinging cats. The more stoic among them said nothing and looked forward to the diving. They were all surprised to find that the *Artemis* was not, strictly speaking, a liveaboard dive boat. They needed to board an entirely different vessel before heading off for the first dive site.

First, a local historian and former captain of a Turkish submarine gave them an exciting and emotional account of the Great War battle. His pleasure at meeting General Hamilton's great nephew was as palpable as much as the younger Ian Hamilton seemed bemused.

The dive boat was a modern steel vessel in the style of a trawler. She was equipped with a crane and an on-board recompression chamber. This thoroughly professional equipment seemed wasted on a crew who took until four in the afternoon to find the first dive site – reputed to be the wreck of "a people-carrier".

It did not help that visibility was rather English and the water temperature likewise. The visitors were equally stunned to find they were diving on what appeared to be nothing more than the equivalent of a ship's lifeboat.

After a particularly disappointing night dive, which turned out to be in no more than 4 m (13 ft) of water, one lady diver took off her tank and threw it down on the deck in disgust, injuring her foot in the process. It was not to be a happy evening.

Overnight, worries about the seaworthiness of *Artemis* were reinforced when it was discovered that she was left to motor devoid of anyone on duty in the wheelhouse and with her helm lashed in position with string. But everyone survived until the next day when they dived a small support vessel, the *Lundy*, and then a reef. They were to wait until the third day before they finally got the opportunity to dive on the wreck of the HMS *Majestic*, off Cape Hellas.

For this, special permission had to be obtained. A Turkish police diver, complete with gun, joined them as escort. It was during the dive briefing that it was first revealed that the *Majestic* had been systematically salvaged by both a German and an Italian company over a period of 12 years. A feeling of foreboding ran through the assembled company. Was this just another wind-up?

It was bemusing to watch the policeman overseeing the divers under water and most wondered what the authorities could possibly be concerned about. The *Majestic* was no longer a wreck. It was just a pile of rubble and unwanted trash left by her earlier salvors.

Surfacing by the dive boat, one of the Brits discovered that during the interim it had been surrounded and penned in by fishing vessels. A torrent of vile and threatening abuse was being levelled at the crew. Not only were they diving in a prohibited zone, it was alleged, they were allowing foreigners to do it too.

The policeman climbed aboard and took off his diving equipment to reveal the word "POLIS" emblazoned across the back of his wetsuit. The fishermen immediately backed off. It was then realised exactly what the policeman's function was.

The next day there was more confusion and misinformation resulting in the group's abandoning any attempt to dive and settling for a day on shore. Returning to the *Artemis* that evening, they found the failure of a pump denied them even a tepid trickle of salty water from their showers. There was a severe failure of the collective sense of humour and the passengers finally mutinied.

Removing any semblance of dignity from people by denying them cleanliness or a good night's sleep can have dramatic results. Some took actions or said words in the heat of the moment that they would later be ashamed of. Some of the women spat vitriol. For a young Alex Venn, representing the trip organiser, it was to be his baptism of fire in the travel industry. Sensibly and not before time, he resettled them in a nearby hotel.

Nevertheless, an air of quiet anticipation hung about the dive boat next morning as they chugged up the Dardanelles Straits towards the last resting place of HMS *Irresistible* close to narrows at Çanakkale. They felt privileged to have finally been given permission to dive this wreck and there were assurances that it had not been salvaged. It lay in some 60 m (197 ft) of water. One diver rigged a twin-set. Others checked pony-bottles or planned the rigging of drop-tanks. Inevitably, disappointment was looming.

"What are the chances of diving this wreck safely?" asked the radio reporter offering his microphone to one of the more experienced divers looking at the current ripping over the site.

"Take your passport with you. You'll probably come up in Russia," was the terse reply. No one took the chance.

The Turkish battleship *Messudiah* was said to lie in calm shallow water. Some later suggested it was near a sewage outfall. Another disappointment eventually turned to anger. Nothing more than a few ribs poked out of the mud – if you could see them.

One veteran diver baldly stated it was the worst diving holiday of his life. Others referred back to the sales brochure. And what did Ian Hamilton make of all this?

On the last day he was seen sitting thoughtfully, eyes narrowed next to the Turkish trenches on the high ground overlooking the landing beaches of Gallipoli.

"Why did the British wait on the beaches for those four hours? If they had pressed on and taken this ground as originally planned, we could have easily beaten the Turks."

It seems a badly serviced and organised dive trip can undo a lot of reconciliation.

THE *IRO* AND ISHIKAWA

It's not often you get a chance to dive a Japanese war wreck in the company of someone that was on it when it was bombed and sunk and can positively identify the vessel.

Every diver has probably heard about the famous World War II action by the American forces that left a fleet of Japanese cargo ships and auxiliaries at the bottom of Truk (Chuuk) Lagoon, but few know that similar military action, in what is now the Republic of Palau, left more than 40 enemy vessels sunk in the lagoons there too.

The fall of Japan's first line of defence in New Guinea, the Solomon Islands, the Marshalls and the Marianas, allowed the Allies to move on to strongholds in Japan's second defensive line. The capture of the Palau Islands became a stepping-stone in General Douglas MacArthur's plan to invade the Philippines. While it is still debated whether the successful capture of the Palau was necessary to protect MacArthur's flank, the battle for the Palau island of Peleliu rates as one of the toughest to be fought during the entire Pacific war.

Japan had not invaded Palau as part of its expansionist plans in the Pacific. It had controlled the islands since the Germans pulled out after the Great War that ended in 1918. As such, it had time to build a virtually unassailable underground fortress of caves and tunnels in

Peleliu beneath its solitary but visible airstrip. The other islands of Palau hid seaplane bases and the infrastructure needed to support a modern naval fleet.

On the last two days of March 1944, an American aircraft carrier attack upon these facilities, a prelude to a full-scale invasion later in the summer, caught many Japanese vessels exposed in the natural harbour of the lagoon areas of Palau. For the Japanese it was a decisive military disaster. The Americans called it "Operation Desecrate One".

Sixty years later, a group of Japanese divers planned to dive to some of the vessels that now lay submerged among the picturesque rock islands.

Someone, remarkably still very much alive at the time, was 86-year-old Tomimatsu Ishikawa, probably the only living survivor from the sinking of the Japanese fleet oiler *Iro*. As a young man, he was the chief engineer of the vessel and had spent most of his adult life aboard the ship until that fateful day. An American bomb that hit the engine room section killed outright all the 15 men working under him.

He told how he had struggled through smoke-filled companionways, stepped over the dead bodies of his shipmates, slipping on oil and blood, before jumping into the lagoon.

Such is the topography of Palau's famous islands – undercut by the activity of marine worms – which take on the appearance of tree-covered mushrooms that are impossible to climb on to from the water. Ishikawa spent several hours in the waters of the lagoon with a handful of other men before being rescued by a patrol craft.

Ishikawa certainly still displayed a massive strength of character even in old age. While visiting Palau in 2004, in his mid-eighties, he went diving and performed a sacred sake, or rice wine, ceremony on the submerged aft deck of his old ship. Michael Rosenthal, the then Minister of Justice, and a young Japanese girl dive-guide accompanied him, together with a number of visiting divers.

It was in memory of fellow seamen who never made it. It was 60 years to the day after their loss.

The old man did this despite his looking extremely uncomfortable under water. Witnesses waiting on the anchor line to get a clear picture of the ancient warrior as he ascended were surprised to see him unwillingly dragged away by his young escort at the last moment and just as he was in sight of the surface. This was for a last touch of the *Iro's* coral encrusted mast. They thought, at that moment, it was obviously something that meant more to her than to him.

It was interesting to compare this old-fashioned Japanese man alongside a new generation of Japanese who seem to have removed any knowledge of what went on during those war years from their collective psyche. Whereas the young Japanese divers saw the events of March 1944 as some sort of unforeseen disaster that was simply a tragedy for the innocent young soldiers of their country, the octogenarian Mr Ishikawa offered an alternative point of view. When asked if he had any regrets about those times, the old chief engineer appeared to baffle those listening by retorting that he wished the Japanese defence had been stronger. He appeared to be somewhat less than contrite.

Back in 1944, when the skies first turned black with American Helldivers and Dauntless dive bombers, the captains of the Japanese vessels cut and ran from their anchorages, attempting to take shelter by keeping close to the steep elevations of the rock islands – but to no avail. They were almost without exception bombed and blasted to extinction.

A footnote to history was that ex-US President George Bush piloted one of the attacking planes. When Palau's President Remengesau later visited America he presented the President's son George W. Bush with an engraved plaque, together with contemporary photographs and modern underwater pictures of what remained of the vessel.

Imagine the chaos and confusion as Operation Desecrate One took on its deadly effect. Ships steaming in all directions, the shouts of the men to action, the boom of anti-aircraft fire, the smoke, the massive detonations as bombs found their targets, the crash of rocks that resulted from those that did not.

Some vessels were so damaged that their wreckage became hard to identify. The *Sata*, another fleet oiler, was sunk within a short distance of the *Iro* and for many years argument raged as to which was which, but Mr Ishikawa was able to positively identify his old home.

The 14 000 ton *Iro* was sunk after a massive detonation in the area of her engine room. The resulting fire burned for a few days before she succumbed to the embrace of the surrounding water. Contrary to information found in many guidebooks, the hull lies perfectly upright in 40 m (130 ft) of water and the top of her aft deck is in around 30 m (100 ft). For some unaccountable reason, visibility becomes poorer as one moves towards the stern. She has massive towers that were used for craning across pipelines and materials to the vessels she fuelled, and these still reach up to within a few metres of the surface. Her funnel lies horizontally where it fell across the deck. A massive gun is mounted on a large radius rotating mounting over her stern. At more than 140 m (455 ft) in overall length, it's hard to fully appreciate this wreck in only one dive. The forward section has superstructure still intact and there is a second large gun mounted in the prow, pointing uselessly downwards. This has a barrel 4 m (14 ft) long and 18 cm (7 in) in diameter. Both guns are completely encrusted in coral.

Only one week before her sinking, a torpedo from submarine USS *Tunny* had hit her in the bow, forward of the bulkheads. She had limped into Palau. That damage, although covered in coral growth, can be clearly seen by divers.

Tomimatsu Ishikawa went home to Japan having survived the sinking of his ship twice within a 60-year period.

THE DISCOVERY OF THE *MARY ROSE*

The rediscovery and raising of the *Mary Rose* were seminal events in the history of nautical archaeology and it was all originally due to amateur divers.

A mateur divers are often responsible for initiating important archaeological work that has led to some very important finds. None can have been more important than the discovery of the wreck of the *Mary Rose* and it can be attributed to the initial diligence and hard work of one man.

Alexander McKee was a keen member of Southsea BSAC, a diving club. Almost he alone was originally responsible for finding the wreck of this now famous ship, which was virtually forgotten about at the time. It had been sunk in a battle that historians had given scant attention to.

With other members of his amateur diving club, he launched what they called Project Solent Ships to locate as many of the historic wrecks as possible, known to lie in the busy estuary of that river and its strait between the Isle of Wight and the mainland. His ambition was to find the wreck of the *Mary Rose*. It was 1965.

A contemporary panorama of the battle known as the Cowdray Engraving conflicted with the received wisdom at the time. Some historians assumed the vessel sank in Portsmouth Harbour while others deduced she had capsized off the Isle of Wight. A lot of water separated the two places.

McKee's industrious and meticulous research eventually revealed an old Admiralty chart on which was clearly marked the position of the wreck. It was half a mile northeast of that of the *Royal George*, a largely forgotten flagship, which sank in the Solent at Spithead in August 1782, and very near the area under water that the members of his dive club had been searching for a year. Little did they know that others had already been salvaging the wreck before them.

John Bevan, a diving historian, wrote recently that while doing salvage work on the *Royal George* in 1834, the pioneering divers, the Deane brothers, had brought up timbers with the Tudor Rose carved on them.

According to Dr Bevan, "John Deane dived on the *Mary Rose* for about two years and brought up a 15 ft section of the mast, bows and arrows, human remains and lots of cannon-balls . . . but as the *Mary Rose* was buried under a thick layer of clay, the dives were not very productive and he abandoned them."

Another year of fruitless searching followed. Alexander McKee had become convinced that the wreck itself was buried under the muddy seabed and it was not until he got hold of a side-scan sonar for use in the search, that luck prevailed. It is said that they found the site of the *Mary Rose* only ten minutes after turning the machine on.

By now archaeologist Margaret Rule had joined the group, still mainly made up of Southsea Branch BSAC divers. She started a Mary Rose Association with a fund into which members put a single pound note each. This fund would be used to cover the expenses expected in excavating the wreck. The enthusiasm was evidently not shared by many of the ordinary public at that time. Bernard Eaton, the owner of UK's *Diver* magazine, launched an appeal for funds in its pages and its readers were the only contributors. They were short of cash but at least the divers now knew where the wreck lay.

The *Mary Rose* was a carrack-type warship of King Henry VIII's Tudor navy. She was one of the first ships able to fire a broadside. In 1545, while leading galleys against a massive French invasion attempt, she capsized and sank in the Solent outside Portsmouth, disappearing under the mud and eventually from public consciousness.

Bernard Eaton later reminiscing, wrote, "It took a further four years to establish the wreck's identity beyond doubt, and the team achieved amazing things during that period. From time to time its members were joined by sport divers from branches such as Southampton, Brighton and the Isle of Wight. Aid also came from the local fire brigade, the Naval Air Command Sub-Aqua Club, the Royal Navy, the Royal Engineers, professional dockyard divers and others.

Under water the divers had to dig laboriously down more than 3.5 m (11 ft) into stiff clay, often by hand, to probe a large area above the invisible wreck. They sometimes worked from borrowed boats in a tideway, in visibilities of less than 30 cm (1 ft) and with surface winds of force 6 and 7. The depth was about 12 m (40 ft), though it was later to become twice as deep. Initially, a plank was discovered 2 m (6 ft) down, which took four cautious days to excavate. Then, in 1969 and 1970, they dug a 27 m (88 ft) long trench and discovered a wrought-iron breech-loading gun, which proved that this was indeed the site of the *Mary Rose*. When, in 1971, almost £10 000 was raised, the greatest underwater salvage saga of all time began in earnest." It was to become a monument to amateur endeavour.

In 1979 Prince Charles became president of the Mary Rose Trust. This was to enable the eventual uncovering, raising and displaying of this historic wreck. It had finally become appreciated that this was one of the most important historical finds ever to be uncovered under water. Both military and naval historians had come to agree that this was a key vessel in the story of the thenceforward rapid development of the wooden ship as a gun platform.

Bernard Eaton continued, "The wreck was covered with a grid of scaffold poles, and each section was numbered. Every volunteer was given a specific project and stations were allocated. My first task as a volunteer was to measure and draw accurately the profile of a

At night, the normally placid little white-tip reef sharks turn into voracious hunters. (White-tips at Night page 7)

Lord Norman Tebbit was rather surprised when a large green turtle decided to bite him! (Lord Tebbit and the Turtle page 11)

This jolly green giant is typical of the frogfish, that prey even on lionfish at Taba, in the Gulf of Aqaba. (The Amazing Frogfish page 14)

Whale sharks are the largest fish in the sea and this one measured around 18m long. A marine park ranger called The Silver Fox is pictured about to undertake an unbelievable stunt. (Galapagos Whale Sharks page 20)

The wreck of the SS *Liberty* lying off the coast of Tulumben in Bali is a favourite overnight roosting place for a hundreds of bumpheaded parrotfish. (Liberty in Bali page 23)

This strange-looking dugong seems oblivious to the maddening crowd of swimmers and snorkellers crowding around it at Marsa Abu Dabab on Egypt's Red Sea coast. (This Dugong Don't Care page 27)

Enormous Australian groupers, now regularly hand fed at Ribbon Reef No. 10 on the Great Barrier Reef, were nicknamed Potato Cod by Stan Waterman. (Fish 'n' Chips at Ribbon Reef No. 10 page 30)

Manta rays are gentle plankton-feeding giants that can be encountered with their accompanying remora fish anywhere in tropical seas. (Manta in the Mist page 34)

Dolphins have a couple of reasons for that enigmatic smile. (Why Dolphins Smile page 37)

Divers who go deep now use rebreathers and exotic gas mixes containing helium rather than take a chance using ordinary air to breathe. (The Call of the Wah! Wah! page 87)

The propellers of the former British destroyer HMS *Myngs* are now covered in vibrantly coloured soft corals. (A British Destroyer Sunk page 104)

Fabio Amaral takes a close look at some of the gauges inside the armoured control centre of the World War II aircraft carrier, the USS *Saratoga*. (USS *Saratoga* CV3 page 108)

Diego Leonardi poses by the enormous multi-bladed prop of the truck-ferry, the *Don Pedro*, now at rest on the seabed outside Ibiza town. (Don Pedro page 115)

A modern rebreather diver investigates the 1876 wreckage of the *Dunraven*, at Beacon Rock, a popular dive site in the Red Sea. (The *Dunraven* and T. E. Lawrence page 118)

A 'Jake' seaplane, sunk at its moorings in Palau during 'Operation Desecrate One'. (The *Iro* and Ishikawa page 128)

A diver makes a video recording of one of the many World War II British motorbikes that formed part of the cargo of the SS *Thistlegorm*, a casualty of a German bomber in the Gulf of Suez in 1941. (The *Thistlegorm* page 136)

Bull sharks are implicated in more attacks on people than almost any other species of shark, but here they get hand-fed for the benefit of visiting divers. (A Lot of Bull page 145)

Highly poisonous lionfish are beautiful to look at, but they represent a hazard to both divers and endemic species in areas of the world where they are intruders. (The Danger of Lionfish page 151)

A saltwater crocodile is quicker off the mark than a racehorse, can leap out of the water up to its hind legs and is very aggressive. It's not something many want to share the water with. (Mauled by a Dinosaur! page 157)

Getting lost at the surface and not found by the boat crew is one of the most serious hazards a diver can face. (Left Stranded in the Sea page 163)

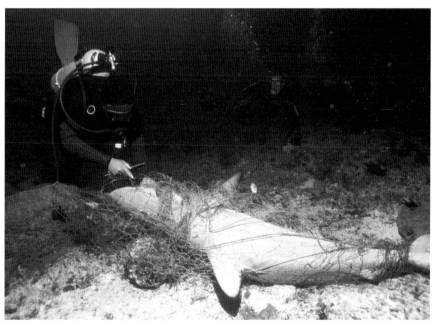

This shark was found by divers trapped in a net. Three experienced divers went back to recover it and made some mistakes in doing so. (Shark in the Net page 167)

Komodo dragons are as big as crocodiles, have a toxic bite and can take down an animal as big as a water buffalo. It's not what you want to meet after finally swimming ashore from being lost at sea. (Photo: Bret Gilliam) (Currents and Dragons page 176)

A shark feed in the Bahamas. The feeder may wear a chainmail suit, but it doesn't absolve them from getting injured. (Bitten by Sharks page 203)

Caribbean Reef sharks are both impressive and beautiful, but they are timid and don't come close to divers unless there is the chance of a free meal. (Bitten by Sharks page 203)

In the shark world, size matters and few come bigger than this six-metre-long tiger shark called Scarface in Beqa Lagoon, Fiji. (Face off a Tiger page 207)

It was Stuart Cove who originally discovered that a diver could put a shark into 'Tonic Immobility' and now shark feeders can demonstrate that all around the world at staged shark feeds. (Tonic Immobility page 211)

The three illusive pre-war Fiat cars that are stowed deep in the hold of the Italian liner, the *Umbria*, scuttled by her crew outside Port Sudan. (Trapped! page 225)

Umberto Pelizarri demonstrates to the author his deep breath-hold diving skills. At one time he held the world-record at 150m deep. (In Search of Free-Diving Records page 238)

Steffi Schwabe, petrologist and underwater explorer, reveals some cave details deep in a flooded Blue Hole in the Bahamas. (Blue Hole Diving page 249)

A diver carefully cleans off the remains of a two-thousand-year-old amphora found concreted into the seabed at a site near to Egypt's Port Berenice. (An Archaeological Find page 253)

gun port at the stern, no easy task as the port was shaped like a staggered funnel.

Armed with a tape measure, pencil and pad inside a plastic bag, I settled down and began to work. A gentle current was running and suddenly I looked down to find that I was standing on a bronze cannon. I also discovered that I was in company with the protruding end of an archer's bow.

What's more, the current gradually exposed a jawbone on a nearby mud ledge. Prince Charles was to visit that same location the next day."

A huge number of medieval artefacts were recovered from where they had been preserved in the mud. Examples of the Tudor longbow had been few and far between before the wreck's discovery. Now there were hundreds. Bernard Eaton recalled, "One recovered chest was full of bows and arrows, an interesting study of one archer's weaponry."

In excess of 14 000 objects were salvaged. Many were immensely important finds and some were unique. The list included numerous guns of all types some of which were remarkably preserved. There was also the earliest known ship's gun carriage and an iron gun that had been produced by some unknown techniques. The *Mary Rose* was finally raised from the mud and out of the water in 1982 and is now in a museum in Portsmouth, much restored and admired by millions of visitors, and it was all down to the initial persistence and hard work of amateur diver Alexander McKee.

THE *THISTLEGORM*

Early dives on what was to become the world's most famous regularly dived wreck.

A s recently as 1992, there were few Egyptians involved in the diving industry in the Red Sea. It had been left in the hands of some battle-hardened Israelis and a few assorted Europeans, foolhardy enough to take their chances with Egyptian bureaucracy, tough climatic conditions and a decidedly third-world supply chain.

Israeli Shimshon Machiah ran a converted Fleetwood trawler called the *Sun Boat*. He ran mainly fishing charters down from Eilat but occasionally transported divers from what was a fledgling diving community. He took his anglers to a site in Sha'ab Ali that he had been shown by Bedouin fishermen, where he believed a World War II wreck lay. Nobody else went there.

Idly browsing through Jacques Cousteau's book *The Living Sea*, which retold the pioneer of scuba-diving's adventures in the fifties in the Red Sea, this author came across a chapter entitled "The *Thistlegorm*". It recounted dives on a World War II wreck, stuffed to the gunnels with motorbikes and trucks and other assorted materials of war. Cousteau told how he stumbled across the wreck while looking out from the underwater observation chamber of his support vessel, the *Calypso*. This was despite the fact that the masts of the wreck would have probably been breaking the surface at that time. When Cousteau dived on the *Thistlegorm* it had been submerged for only 11 years.

Coincidentally, at the same time as the author had been reading Cousteau's book, another one-time, Red Sea dive-guide, David Wright, had been reading an old copy of *National Geographic* magazine, also with a story of the *Thistlegorm*. Cousteau, ever the great storyteller, recounted meeting a Napoleon wrasse as big as a truck on the wreck. David was told about Shimshon's wreck story. The two compared notes, put two and two together and got a chart position from Shimshon, but, of course, in those days GPS was in its infancy, and so were GPS receivers. It wasn't that simple.

Without a precise and proper position for the wreck, they decided to drag for it in the general area with a small anchor on the end of a long line. Eventually they struck and were able to confidently enter the water.

The two were amazed. Not only because it turned out to be such a big wreck, not just because it sat upright, not because of what it contained in the way of cargo, but because of the marine life it had attracted.

It was smothered from stem to stern with colourful soft corals resplendent in crimson reds and bright orange. The stern was home to literally hundreds of large Red Sea groupers. In places they looked like so many pigs crammed together at a market. A huge school of barracuda hung toothily but motionless over the deck in the current. Black-tip sharks skulked around the sandy seabed.

Hold covers floated off and it was simple to drop down and find the cargo was more or less intact. It was a time capsule from the desert war of 1941. Apart from a couple of bikes that had evidently been lifted to the surface by the Cousteau team and then simply tossed back, everything was ship-shape and in order. Row upon row of BSA, Norton and Triumph motorbikes were stacked upon truck after AEC Matador or Bedford truck. The saddles of the bikes had rotted but their fuel tanks were intact and their toolkits still sat where they were carried, under their seats. There was little of that wanton destruction seen today, with truck's windshields broken, steering wheels and wipers missing, bikes with fuel tanks smashed as a result of the work of modern underwater souvenir hunters. There were the wings of Gloucester Gladiators and, among other less easily identified material, the huge gearbox cases from tank transporters and some armoured cars built on Rolls-Royce chassis.

Enfield 303 rifles in less than perfect working order, were revealed in clusters by the fact that the wooden boxes that had contained them were rotted and no more. The same could be said of piles of rubber boots that had originally been contained in cardboard. There were valve radios piled high. The utensils in the galley were as they had been left when they were first immersed.

The decks carried railway wagons and engine tenders, although the explosions that sank the ship had blown off the massive Stannier freight locomotives from where they had been chained. The remains of their smoke boxes and front bogies lay forlornly either side of the ship on the seabed where they had come to rest. Two minesweeping drones were still stowed neatly.

Behind the central superstructure was an area of turmoil and chaos. This is where the German bomb had struck that fateful night. It had left nothing but twisted metal and a great heap of steel ammunition boxes mostly bearing 25-pound shells and some very much larger for heavy artillery. A couple of Bren gun carriers were recognisable by their tracks. Beyond that, the stern was twisted to one side, but a heavy calibre machine gun and a more conventional ship's gun, still clung to the deck, not a single shot fired the night the vessel was hit.

It was 1992 when it was first rediscovered and since then it has now become probably the most often dived shipwreck in the world.

PART FIVE

Dangerous Animals

CONGER ATTACK!

A quick-thinking instructor saves the day after an unexpected attack by a conger eel.

Wham! A great thick silvery eel, around 2 m (6.5 ft) long and with a girth like a telegraph pole, hurtled out of the feeding frenzy and hit the girl kneeling innocently on the sand, full in the face. Instinctively, she had turned her face away and caught the teeth of the monster full in the right cheek. Blood and subcutaneous fat gushed from the hole, along with some bubbles of air. She was unable to inhale from her scuba regulator because of the leak in her face and was instantly in danger of drowning.

Thinking quickly, the dive guide dropped the camera he was holding and shot over to her immediately. It was obvious what the problem was and he closed up the hole in her cheek with his right hand while gripping her securely by the straps of her equipment with the other. He knew what he had to do.

They started to ascend. It was obvious that she didn't really understand what had happened. They had 33 m (107 ft) to ascend at around 10 m (30 ft) per minute in order to avoid the complications of decompression sickness. That's more than three minutes. It was a long time.

He was aware that should she suddenly start to panic, she might struggle and strike out for the surface. Holding her breath, she might be in danger of rupturing a lung, although with a hole in her cheek, her airway would be open and that would be unlikely.

Gripping her tightly and holding that cheek closed, he never lost eye contact with her. The three minutes ascent time gave him time to think over what had happened.

In the centre of the channel that separates Mallorca at its south-westerly point from the dramatic island of Dragonera, there lie the sunken remains of a wooden fishing boat. It isn't much of a wreck, just a mess of broken wood, torn nets and a small diesel engine with its transmission. If it were on land it would have amounted to nothing more than a pile of rubbish, something that you might pass at the roadside. Under water, things are different.

The seabed of the channel is a featureless sandy desert. The current gently pushes along through the gap at Punta Tramontana and gradually fades as the channel widens toward the seaside village of San Telmo, now known as Sant Elm. This wreck – this pile of junk – represents the only habitat around and had become a magnet for the Mediterranean marine life that needed somewhere to hide during the daylight hours.

Predatory scorpion fish lay in wait for the unwary black chromis fish that flitted around the wreck like so many bees. As many as 40 moray eels would hide among the broken spars and netting that formed the wreck, gulping down oxygenated water like so many silent barking dogs. Mediterranean morays are snake-like in appearance. The dive guide used to call it his snake-pit dive.

More fearsome were the conger eels. These muscular animals have thick silvery bodies, with massive heads and a mouthful of teeth. They rarely show more than their head from the cavities they hide in during daylight hours, with big yellow and black nocturnal eyes staring defiantly at anyone who dares to approach. Here, things were different.

The dive guide regularly took along a screw-top jar filled with fresh sardines and was in the habit of carefully offering them one-at-a-time to the biggest eels. It had to be done with care and concentration, but the result was that these eels would slither from the safety of their hideouts and swim round in open water like so many airborne silvery pythons, a very spectacular sight indeed. He'd save the event for the last dive of a series so that visiting divers would go home with something special to remember. So what went wrong this time?

One day, the dive guide found himself escorting three attractive female divers and after they'd experienced the snake-pit dive that morning, they pleaded for the chance to do it again before they left the island to go home. One of the girls had asked if she could feed the "pussycats".

Men have a failing in that their judgement can often become impaired when it comes to dealing with attractive young women. He agreed. After all, it would give him the opportunity to take some pictures with his underwater camera.

So, once again later that day, they were down on the seabed at 33 m (107 ft) deep, with their boat at the surface above them securely moored by anchor. They were ready to feed the eels. The main difference was that it was late afternoon and one of the girls was going to do the feeding.

Eels hunt at night and so they become quite aggressively hungry by the end of the long Mediterranean summer day. When the divers knelt by the wreck in preparation for the staged eel feed, several of the bigger eels swam out to meet them. The girl was obviously daunted by the prospect and taking the lid off the glass jar, shook all of the fresh sardines in one mass out into the water. This precipitated mayhem. Any element of control had been lost.

A gaggle of snake-like morays competed with half a dozen massive congers to get their share of the bounty. Congers cannot hover in the water. They must swim round, but because of the writhing nature of their swimming action, it's difficult to anticipate where they are heading next. It was a feeding frenzy. It was like an aerial snake pit and something that even Indiana Jones had never had to contend with.

One girl retreated several metres upwards to view the melee from above. Another retreated to watch from further away, kneeling on the sandy seabed. The girl with the now empty glass jar seemed mesmerised by what was happening. Her long hair was flowing around her face, driven by the turbulence generated by so many swimming eels. The dive guide went over to her to drag her from the obvious danger of so many snapping mouths.

It was at this moment that a single big conger eel had broken away from the pack. Attracted by the silver metal front of the kneeling girl's regulator, the eel tried to grab it, obviously confusing it with a silver sardine, and biting her face instead.

The three-minute climb from seabed to surface seemed to last a lifetime. Once they made fresh air, it became apparent that the casualty was unaware of what had actually happened. She felt as if she had simply been punched in the face. The dive guide played down the situation and got her into the boat, breaking out the first-aid kit and getting her to hold a dressing against the wound. The other girl divers retrieved the dropped camera and made their way back up to the boat too. It was a quick drive to the Red Cross station for antibiotics and stitches. The girl was left with a small crescent-shaped scar on her cheek and a story to tell years later that some may disbelieve!

A LOT OF BULL

Bull sharks are implicated in more attacks on people than almost any other species of shark.

"Bull sharks are rarely seen by divers, there are very few photographs of them available, and I've just shot 10 rolls of film on them," exclaimed Jeremy Stafford-Deitch excitedly, as he climbed yet again from the water to reload his camera.

He was at Walkers Cay, a tiny spot in the Abaco chain of the Bahamas. It's a place well known for its "chumsicle" shark feeds, when up to 200 assorted black-tip, Caribbean reef and nurse sharks, plus the occasional hammerhead, turn up to feed from a barrel of frozen fish scraps suspended in the water. It has delighted hundreds of watching divers in the past. It makes for fantastic diving, swimming round in the company of such predators and in such large numbers, but this experience with bull sharks was very different indeed.

With him was Swiss-born Dr Erich Ritter, shark behaviourist from the Hofstrar University (Long Island, NY), but based in Miami, and Gary Adkison, shark enthusiast and manager of Walkers Cay marina and diving centre. They had discovered that bull sharks congregated in numbers in the murky water next to the island's airstrip, a place now appropriately named Shark Beach.

Jeremy Stafford-Deitch, author of best-selling books about sharks and founder of the UK-based Shark Trust, was there to take photographs of bull sharks for his next book, *Sharks of the Caribbean*.

"Aren't they just like Caribbean reef sharks but bigger?" he was asked.

"The easy way to differentiate between these species," offered Dr Ritter, "is that Caribbean reefs are known as ridgeback sharks. Bull sharks don't have that feature. A lot of people call the bigger Caribbean reefs 'bulls' but they are wrong."

"Wait until you get in and see these animals," Jeremy suggested. "Once you've seen a bull shark you'll never forget it. There are more than a dozen big bull sharks here and we get in and swim with them. This is almost unknown in the shark world."

Bull sharks typically favour the murky conditions found at river mouths and in harbours. The habitat at Shark Beach had grassy sand flats beyond the rocks, and discarded rubble and old iron that had been tipped there. Fishermen had been throwing their fish cleanings there for generations. The water was so shallow the divers could stand up in it. Fins, mask and snorkel were all that was necessary, and so equipped they slipped off the rocks with their cameras to join the big dark shapes that already split the surface with their massive dorsal fins. Dr Ritter was armed with a video camera and ebullient Texan Gary Adkison stood on the shore ready with a trash bin full of unwanted fish parts recovered from the marina's fish-cleaning room.

"These are the biggest bulls I've ever seen," exclaimed Dr Ritter on first seeing them. "I reckon the girls, the big females, must be around 2.5 m (9 ft) long and weigh in at 273 kg (600 lb) plus each. Imagine the size of the male that could pin one of these down."

Some of the divers couldn't help thinking that they had never noticed the genitalia of sharks so clearly before. The claspers of the males were bright white and contrasted strangely with the dark grey of the surrounding skin. The cloacas of the females seemed over-large and gaping. Then there were their little yellow piggy-eyes.

They each had a very broad-based dorsal fin and virtually no fin markings. What was very obvious was the enormous bulk of their bodies; their tremendous girth.

"What's very interesting is that bull sharks have the most fearsome reputation for shark attacks, yet you can flick a hand at them and they will retreat," observed Jeremy. "The first day when I was here on my own I was very cautious. I had to get out of the water when 14 of them starting competing for the bait. It got a bit hectic."

They counted only 10 that day.

Gary carefully lobbed the bait so that it was just ahead of their cameras.

Jeremy questioned if they would get stomach ache from eating so much smelly fish. Dr Ritter explained that sharks have very powerful bacteria living permanently in their mouths. These bacteria overpower any foreign bugs. He explained that if you were to survive the massive loss of blood from a shark bite, the next problem you would encounter would be the massive secondary infection from these powerful bacteria. Gary remembered a shark-bite survivor going down with a life-threatening, pneumonia-like infection.

Fully grown bull sharks are big. Their massive girth makes them look ponderous and slow – that is until a piece of dead fish hits the surface and comes floating down. Then they move extremely quickly indeed. The divers found that if they snorkelled down towards the sinking bait, camera at the ready and careful not to get there before a competing shark, they could get a dramatic photograph of that important moment; a moment that happened so quickly they often missed the shot of the open jaws, the shaking head and searing teeth.

Other fish were in there feeding too. There was a little needle-fish holding his own and some octopus that grabbed anything that came within reach and disappeared under cover of the rock and junk strewn on the bottom. One octopus took advantage of one diver and climbed his leg to his groin in order to get a better opportunity.

From time to time another species of shark would turn up and compete for the food. A solitary lemon shark looked very scrawny by comparison. They always thought nurse sharks had bulk until they saw one in the company of these sumo wrestlers of the shark fraternity. A feisty black-tip looked like a pretty little toy next to them.

"If you speared a live fish these giants would go completely bananas. You would not get out of the water alive. These ones have quickly learned to recognise the sound of the fish scraps hitting the surface and they have learned to feed at the surface in the couple of days we have been doing this," offered Jeremy. "Erich is completely fearless of course."

Dr Ritter had many theories, the pursuit of the proof of which he was prepared to risk his personal safety. This included floating closely over a dead fish and allowing a big shark to take it from under him. The sharks usually approached in pairs.

"We think they must be able to communicate in order to coordinate their actions."

Others were not so sure. Some thought they just found it convenient to hunt in packs.

"A bull shark needs to eat four percent of its own body weight in fish each day. That means some of these animals are eating 20–30 lb. This bunch probably consumes 200 lb. They seem to feed in groups of pairs and although they can make 30 mph they are very conservative with their energy," Erich usefully informed onlookers.

"I don't do what I do because I'm a daredevil. I want to show that you can swim with notorious species. We want to find out what people do to trigger the wrong reaction. We do stupid things like putting fish blood on our hands to test our theories. The shark is a really smart animal. When you lose your fear you begin to see what it really is."

"Does pissing in the water cause shark attack?" someone asked after we had been in the water for more than three hours.

Dr Ritter regarded his questioner with the whimsical expression of a man who was familiar with the delight of hot urine in a cold wetsuit.

"That's complete rubbish!" he replied eventually with a smile. "We are trying to develop a body language system to build a bridge to the animal, to try to trigger favourable reactions rather than the wrong ones.

We have to do this with species with a known record for attacks – reputed man-eaters. As you have experienced, we can swim with a pack of hungry sharks and do it safely. There really is nothing to worry about."

"Tell me more about this communication business," another asked.

"First of all, it takes some thought to realise that sharks are not fishes. Birds are more closely related to mammals than sharks are to fishes. If they were related it was more than 500 million years ago. A shark's brain related to its body weight outranks many mammals. We are out here (in the water) every day and yet we know so little. A shark sees well, it hears well and it has a well-developed sense of smell. It can also pick up differing frequencies of vibrations. We think the lateral line system is used to communicate between sharks. They may not be super-intelligent but there is good evidence to show they communicate. After 500 million years of evolution, to become the apex predator, the shark surely cannot just rely only on receiver mechanisms."

They certainly seemed to work in pairs, even if one of them got none of the fish scraps Gary threw in. It was found that if a diver presented a small frontal area by swimming non-competitively towards the sharks as they approached a bait, he was in better shape to get a good photograph than if he swam vertically, breathing through a snorkel and holding the camera at waist level. This went some way to enhancing some personal beliefs that animals under water, judge size and therefore threat, by the vertical height of another animal rather than the length.

"World shark research started off around trying to develop effective shark repellents," Dr Ritter continued. "Most shark scientists study pickle jars because they are afraid to get in the water. They believe old myths. It's weird when you don't share this fear because you quickly discover that sharks are not mindless monsters."

Jeremy Stafford-Deitch, inimitably English and a gentle giant, offered his own point of view.

"Erich has a much stronger sense than I that they are not dangerous. Period. I was very cautious but once I saw their focus was the bait we were feeding them, I quickly realised that in that situation they were not a threat to humans. However, Erich obviously has not seen them frenzy up the way I did on my first day. In profile they look a bit like tiger sharks. I find this interesting because both species enjoy a very generalistic diet. They are very catholic in their tastes. That said, there are many so-called shark experts who don't get wet. I don't know how you can have any appreciation of these animals unless you go under water and interact with them."

Dr Ritter was attacked by one of these sharks during filming for television at a later date. He lost a part of his leg and nearly his life. The attack was later shown on national television.

THE DANGER
OF LIONFISH

Why this beautiful looking predator is dangerous for more than just its virulent poison.

L
ouise Murray knows that lionfish can be dangerous. She was
stung by one during a night dive in the Red Sea, while diving
from a boat in the Sudan. Farzi Mireskandari knows too. She
was stung by one while diving from the shore at Taba in the Gulf of
Aqaba. Apart from the different geographical locations, both events
bore a remarkable similarity.

Louise was taking pictures with her underwater camera in the dark.
Farzi swam through a thick cloud of glassfish for the benefit of another
underwater photographer. Glassfish are a major prey for lionfish.

Both women let their hands come into contact with the poisonous
spines of this bizarre looking, yet commonly encountered Indo-Pacific
fish, and both experienced the same sharp, jabbing pain.

It takes time to ascend from a dive, climb back aboard a boat or
make it to the shore, remove your diving equipment and seek medical
help, no matter how urgently you make it. By this time both ladies

were suffering an excruciating pain that had moved up through their hand and was tracking along their forearms.

The venom of lionfish is contained within the rigid spines of their feathery-looking dorsal, anal and pectoral fins. Each spine has a pair of lateral grooves along the outer two-thirds of its length and these contain the glandular tissue that produces the venom.

Medical books recommend consulting a doctor. For these two women, no doctors were available. Some books advise against any hot-water methods but nothing else was available.

By now the pain had become so severe and was tracking up through the arm towards the chest – something had to be done and done quickly. In both cases it was decided to immerse the affected areas in hot water in an attempt to break down the toxins.

Bowls of hot water were produced and each of the ladies submerged their arms. The water was made as hot as they could bear. As soon as they had become accustomed to its temperature, the water was topped up with more, hotter water. This gradual increase in the heat of the water eventually had the effect of "boiling" their hand, forearm and part of the upper arm and it seemed to be working! The pain of the sting was overriding the pain of the water and both ladies encouraged their helpers to add water that was hotter. The pain stopped tracking before it went past the elbow. Gradually, it started to recede. After about an hour or so the pain had almost gone. Both women were left with pink and crinkly hands that recovered within a 36-hour period. Both thought the treatment had been worth it. Neither suffered any further symptoms.

The tropical medicine textbooks tell us that envenomation (a sting) results in an immediate burning pain that rapidly spreads and may include the whole limb. The area around the puncture site reddens and swells. This oedema may last for several days. Although it is painful, a sting from a lionfish is not as dangerous as is often supposed. However, the symptoms of nausea, vomiting, heart palpitations and general feelings of weakness are usually physical reactions to the pain.

Lionfish are common in the Red Sea. They may also be encountered in large parts of the Indo-Pacific region. These attractive looking feathery fish are not normally considered dangerous and are favourite subjects of the underwater photographer. There is one part of the world where they are becoming very dangerous indeed but not because of their venomous sting.

Lionfish have started to invade the Caribbean and the Atlantic through the Bahamas north past Florida. Divers have even seen one as far north as the Carolinas of the USA. This part of the marine world normally has a range of tropical fish species quite different to the Indo-Pacific, but the lionfish has arrived. Nobody knows how it happened. Some blame it on a Florida aquarium damaged in a hurricane a decade before. Others think tropical fish-keepers released some of their pets into the sea when they grew too large for their fish tanks. Even more think that their young were carried in the ballast tanks of ships. It doesn't matter now. The fact is that the species has crossed the Atlantic and, since 1992 when they were first encountered in the waters off Florida, they have spread north to Bermuda, the Bahamas and drifted south past Cuba to the islands of the Caribbean proper. Some say they are now off the coast of Venezuela. Originally, genetic tests on those caught had confirmed that all were the descendants of only two original fish. More recently it has been discovered that two different species of Indo-Pacific lionfish are involved.

So, what's the problem?

The difference here is that they have no natural predators. A female can lay two million eggs each year. These float in a jelly-covered bundle that evidently other Caribbean fish do not find palatable. The eggs hatch after around 45 days. They are voracious predators. They can swallow other fishes up to two-thirds their own length. They hover effortlessly in the water, whooshing water out through their mouths to simulate a current. Small fishes tend to swim into a current. The fry of other fishes simply swim up into the lionfish's open jaws.

Invasive species such as lionfish upset the balance of nature. Free of the predators, diseases and parasites that would normally keep their numbers in check, their populations are booming at the expense of indigenous fishes. It seems they are destined to decimate life on the reefs of the Caribbean area and they carry a well-documented venomous sting that's hazardous to people too, although neither Louise nor Farzi have had further ill effects from their unfortunate experiences.

THE TERROR OF
THE IRUKANDJI

Snakes, stonefish and scorpions notwithstanding, the most poisonous animal in the sea is a tiny, invisible jellyfish.

When people first go into the sea to swim, they are naturally concerned about what animals might be sharing the water with them. They worry about sharks, toothy barracuda and poisonous animals like snakes or stonefish. The oceans still teem with life despite the activities of industrialised fishermen. That said, sea turtles have become an endangered species and it is they that feed on jellyfish. The result is a worldwide explosion in jellyfish populations that have made sea bathing an often alarmingly painful experience. It gets worse.

For generations, the aboriginal people of the Irukandji tribe have spoken of an evil presence in the waters off their coast on Australia's Great Barrier Reef, that can torture with unthinkable agony. They believed this pain was caused by a devil inhabiting the ocean. It formed a scourge that today bears the tribe's name, the Irukandji syndrome. The syndrome was given its name in 1952 by Hugo Flecker, after the people who live in Palm Cove, north of Cairns, Australia, where stings are sadly common.

THE TERROR OF THE IRUKANDJI

In March 2002, an American tourist was snorkelling through the pristine waters of the reef near Hamilton Island in the Whitsundays, when he received a tiny sting. He couldn't see anything that might have caused it. After some minutes a headache set in and he retreated back to the boat. After another 10 minutes, the pain began to spread with severe muscle cramps until he could no longer control his movements.

Airlifted to a hospital, the doctors were almost helpless in what they could do for him. There is no anti-venom for the Irukandji syndrome. They could only give him powerful painkillers to help alleviate the agony but he "continually climbed the stairs of pain". Within two weeks he was dead from a brain haemorrhage. He had been killed by a tiny, almost invisible jellyfish weighing less than a few grams.

A few months later, a second tourist suffered the same fate after being stung in the sea near Port Douglas. He suffered headache, shooting pains in the muscles, chest, abdomen and back. Other symptoms included a feeling of nausea and vomiting. What usually killed the victims of the Irukandji jellyfish was hypertension and heart failure due to the excruciating and continuing pain.

These animals had been undiscovered until 1964 when Dr Jack Barnes, an emergency room doctor, who had attempted to treat numerous people suffering the same, proved their existence. He routinely searched the coastal waters near Cairns, Queensland, Australia, until he found what he was looking for. Nobody believed that such a modest-looking creature could throw such a deadly punch. To prove his case he let one sting himself, the local lifeguard and his son. Within the hour all three were in hospital with Irukandji syndrome but luckily all three survived. In honour of his dedication, the jellyfish were named *Carukia barnesi*.

Unlike the well-known and almost equally deadly box jellyfish, the Irukandji jellyfish can be found in deeper waters offering a hazard to divers and snorkellers that don't wear a full covering of neoprene, despite the waters being very warm.

Since 1964, as the scientific community became better informed, more and more cases have been linked to this inauspicious-looking jellyfish, but only recently has it been discovered that the stings of at least six different species of jellyfish can cause the illness.

Divers are usually immune to such attacks. They tend to go into the water clad in rubber, often with hood and gloves. If you think that that can keep you safe – think again. You may think that you're safe if you never dive near the region where the most stings have occurred, such as in North Queensland – think again.

The news gets more disturbing. Cases of Irukandji syndrome have cropped up far beyond the warm, tropical waters of the Far East and the Pacific. An American military combat diver on a routine training mission in Florida, completely covered in neoprene from head to toe, apart from maybe a small area of cheek between his regulator and his mask, got stung and suffered Irukandji syndrome. This was in the coastal waters of the USA. There have since been reported cases in Japan and even one in the rather cold waters off the coast of the UK. It seems these jellyfish can exist almost anywhere!

MAULED BY A DINOSAUR!

Don't worry about the sharks. They've all been eaten by the crocodile!

S altwater crocs are the largest, most aggressive of all the crocodiles. They can outrun a racehorse over a short distance. They can leap out of the water vertically up to their hind legs. They have a reaction time 60 times quicker than a man's, and they are so aggressive they will attack any other saltwater crocodile that comes near including a potential mate. They are not the sort of animal you'd want to meet while diving, but they range large distances across the north of Australia and around Papua New Guinea and Eastern Indonesia. David Shem-Tov had an unfortunate experience with one, but he lived to tell the tale.

David was diving in the Raja Ampat, an archipelago of islands that are close to the Bird's Head peninsular of West Papua, with his friend Chus Barrientos when he heard him shouting through his regulator and saw him finning backwards furiously. At the surface a mere 6 m (20 ft) away, David saw a crocodile swimming fast and in his direction.

He held his breath and froze, hoping the animal would not notice him, but it was too late. It dived down towards him.

David and Chus were diving in a narrow shallow channel where uniquely, fan corals flourished near the surface and archerfish hunted insects under the mangroves. They were with a local Papuan guide, who had suddenly swum away briskly into deeper water. This is David's first-hand account.

"This was when I heard Chus' shout. Within five seconds of seeing the crocodile, I was struck. Springing back, I narrowly avoided having my skull crushed by its jaws.

Its claws tore the mask from my face and the regulator from my mouth so violently that my chin was lacerated and part of one incisor broken off.

Only the thin neoprene of my wetsuit stopped my torso being shredded.

The crocodile snapped again. The jaws locked on my right arm and I was pulled down. Everything became a blur, but it was obvious that the crocodile was trying to drown me. I could feel its massive strength, yet there was no pain."

From a distance, the dive guide saw the crocodile sinking back down, swinging its head from side to side, shaking David like a puppet in its jaws. The animal was huge. Later, a renowned crocodile expert, Dr Graham Webb from Darwin, Australia, estimated that it was probably an adult male of more than 4 m (13 ft) long and weighing probably 500 kg (1100 lb).

Chus headed down to try to save his friend by first attempting to prise the animal's muzzle open by pulling at the rubbery flesh under its lower jaw.

"It had a scaly back that felt like a tree trunk," he said afterwards. Trying to discourage the animal by gouging at its eyes had no effect and he returned disheartened to the surface.

Luckily, crocodiles kill by drowning their victims and David, trapped by its jaws, could still breathe from his aqualung. Down below, he was in a state of shocked disbelief. The prospect of encountering a crocodile in the water, let alone being attacked by one, hadn't occurred to him. The sight of these terrifying jaws lunging at him had felt almost unreal. He quickly snapped out of it. The shock was replaced by a powerful sensation of heightened awareness and clarity. There was no panic. After some moments, the crocodile suddenly let go of his right forearm and bit on to his left hand, pulling him down the sloping bottom to a depth of 10 m (33 ft).

Because his right arm was covered in the neoprene of his suit and he was also able to breathe without struggling, the crocodile may have been uncertain as to what it first had got hold of, but as he was not wearing gloves, the exposed flesh of his left hand was now bleeding.

Until then, David's thoughts had been to hold on as best he could until help arrived. He tried to keep calm to slow down his breathing but knew that after the previous hour's diving the remnants of air in his tank would not last long.

It then occurred to David that nobody was coming to help him. He realised that he was on his own and was going to have to fight for his life.

He couldn't release his left hand from those brutal jaws. They were firmly clamped shut.

"I then stabbed my index and middle fingers into the crocodile's eye. To my surprise, there was no resistance. It felt soft, as if I had plunged them into a bowl of jelly. It was probably the same eye that Chus had injured earlier.

I dug in ferociously."

He remembered this going on for a while before the reptile abruptly released his hand and swam away. The prey was causing too much trouble so it reluctantly withdrew. David shot to the surface and Chus dragged him into the boat. The attack had lasted 16 minutes.

First aid applied, a single suture to each of several wounds and antibiotics courtesy of one of the other passengers on their liveaboard, and David retired to rest in the wheelhouse to get over the ordeal. The dive guide later regretted not entering the water to help but they both knew that he could have done very little and they both could have been killed. No apology was required. At the time of the attack there had been 20 divers in the water. The saltwater crocodile is thought to be so rarely encountered in Indonesian waters that it is legally protected, but another diver had experienced a lucky escape from another smaller animal at the same site four months earlier.

PART SIX

Near Misses and the Not So Near

LEFT STRANDED
IN THE SEA

Divers can have a great time under water but the fun stops when they find their boat has gone without them.

D ive guide John Henry discovered they were alone on surfacing from a dive on a remote reef in the outer reaches of Sudanese waters. There was no inflatable and no vessel, big or small, in sight. The view all the way to the horizon was alarmingly unoccupied. He had surfaced with a dozen Italian passengers who were intent on having a good time. He laughed hollowly and said that this was always happening. "The boat would come back in a moment," he told them but in his heart he knew that things were bad.

The reefs around Dahrat Abid, near the border with Eritrea, come up from ocean depths like vertical pillars. Anchoring a boat means using two reef anchors laid on the top of the reef, with lines in a Y-shape formation and the vessel in the lee of the prevailing wind. Dive boats in Egypt that need to moor close to a reef do it all the time.

The captain, who was not the usual captain but one that had been brought in at the last moment for the trip by the owner, had better ideas. He sent a deckhand diving down to 40 m (130 ft) deep to loop a steel wire hawser round any convenient protrusion of rock from the reef wall. Then a heavy rope or "warp" was lowered and attached to this fixed point – that is how he liked to anchor the boat.

The vessel weighed a couple of hundred tonnes and would exert a mighty tug on this anchor line, subject to the never-ending action of wind and waves. It was inevitable that at some time the hawser would cut through the soft coral rock, but usually not quicker than the duration of a dive.

This time things were different. The hawser had not cut through the rock but the whole coral head had come adrift from the reef wall. Allowing for the angle of attack, this means that the main vessel now was drifting with a tonne of rock dangling from its mooring line about 80 m (260 ft) below. It was too much for the winch. The effect was to make the 30 m (100 ft) motor yacht impossible to steer.

The Captain was unwilling to cut through an expensive four-inch thick warp and let the rock go free. He needed all the mooring line he could keep for the long months he foresaw ahead, operating far from normal supply lines and in the southern Red Sea.

The divers' pick-up boat was used to push the bow of the main vessel away from collision with other reefs while the deckhand had to descend to 80 m (260 ft) to cut through the steel wire hawser with a hacksaw.

This took time, especially when you consider the decompression requirements for that deep a dive, and it took more than one dive. Several hours passed while the deckhand either worked away below, or lay on the deck exhausted and trying to make the most of any surface interval. The vessel with the inflatable pick-up boat in attendance, drifted further and further away from where it had started.

Meanwhile, John Henry had told his charges to inflate their BCs (buoyancy controls) and float in a relaxed manner, being careful to ensure they kept close to the reef in the lee of the wind. He told them to lie back and enjoy the Sudanese sun and get a tan. He had no way of knowing what had happened so he regaled them with as many funny stories he could think of from his home country Scotland, and thanked the Lord he could remember so much of Billy Connolly's performances. The Italians laughed and joked and generally stayed in good humour. After a few hours things started looking bleak. People ran out of things to talk about and John started to quietly talk to the Lord about a few subjects other than a vulgar, if very funny, Scottish comedian.

Eventually, back at the boat, the rock was freed from the anchor line, the vessel's engines started and she was driven back to where she should have been. A group of divers with very sunburned faces were picked up, yet the Captain refused to tell them what had happened, though the crew soon told John in private. They were lucky. They stayed by the reef and the crew of their vessel knew where to find them.

Six Japanese divers were lost in the strong currents and heavy seas near Pelelui Island, Palau. Even though the people in their boat knew that they were there somewhere, they couldn't pick them out in the unexpectedly rough water. Other dive boats joined the search. One of the Japanese divers wrote (in Japanese) on her message slate, "We can see you looking for us but you can't see us." Their lifeless bodies were found floating, still in their diving equipment, a few days later.

The Lonergans were not lucky either. They were a recently married young couple from Baton Rouge, Louisiana, USA. Tom and Eileen booked a diving trip in Queensland on a boat called *Outer Edge*. They had recently completed work for the Peace Corps on the island of Tuvalu and were going on to do more work in Fiji. In between they had treated themselves to some time off to dive on Australia's Great Barrier Reef.

They were an intimate couple that kept themselves to themselves, so they had no real conversations with any of the other passengers during the long journey out to Agincourt Reef. It was probably because of this, that their absence was unnoticed back on board when, thinking the dives were over, the captain set off back to the mainland.

It was not until two days later that the couple was known to be missing. It was when their bag with their belongings was discovered on the boat. A huge air and sea search ensued over the next three days but they were never found. Some of their diving gear was discovered washed up on a beach that was many miles away from where they first entered the water.

Later, a fisherman came across a diver's message slate, the type more normally used for communicating between divers under water. On it was written in partly obliterated pencil, "Monday Jan 26. To anyone who can help us. We have been abandoned at Agincourt Reef by mv. Outer Edge Jan 98 3pm. Please come to rescue us before we die. Help!!!"

Several theories were mooted at the time that they had variously staged their disappearance or committed suicide. Their bank accounts were not touched, neither was any life insurance claimed. Eileen's father, John Hains, was pretty sure that the couple became dehydrated and disoriented and in the end drowned. The coroner dismissed any idea that they had committed suicide or faked their disappearance and formally charged the boat's skipper, Jack Nairn, but he was later judged to be not guilty. The 2003 movie *Open Water* was based on the story, only their names were changed to Daniel Kintner and Susan Watkins.

SHARK IN THE NET

Three very experienced divers had messed up, each in his own way, but they survived to tell the tale.

The currents around the Indonesian islands of Komodo and Rinca can be very strong indeed. So strong in fact that many vessels used by divers as liveaboards cannot make headway if the tidal flow is against them. A couple of years ago, a group of divers foolishly left their boat at anchor and went missing. Some were British and the television news in the UK gave the event a lot of coverage. They were eventually discovered some time later on Rinca, fending off with rocks the predatory advances of a Komodo dragon, a species of giant lizard so fearsome that a toxic bite can take down a water buffalo.

Most people dive from liveaboards. Some years earlier, a group of divers from one such liveaboard dived at a site where they encountered a fairly large, sandbar shark caught up in a discarded fishing net. Back on the boat and hearing of this sighting, Matt, the American captain, decided that it would be right to devote a dive to freeing this animal. Matt, his Australian ship's mate Zane, and a very experienced diving journalist present on that particular trip, decided to undertake this mission while the other guest divers dived elsewhere. The plan was to drop them from the pick-up boat before it went on to another site.

All three of them quickly dropped over the side. Alas, this was in the early days of BCs with integrated weight systems. In those days, they relied on Velcro to keep the weights in place and unfortunately Velcro lost its sticking properties under the influence of seawater and a tropical sun. As the journalist duck-dived down he beheld his weight pockets tumbling down below him and soon disappearing out of sight. He surfaced to see the pick-up boat heading off at high speed.

He couldn't stay at the surface because the ripping current would carry him for many miles before the boat came back, so he headed down, pulling himself down the reef by judicious use of his reef hook. He soon found the other two with Matt hard at work on the net, cutting a section of it away in order to free the shark.

It was tough work in the strong current and it was relatively deep at about 30 m (98 ft). After some time, during which Zane seemed to do little to help, the shark was free and the journalist was surprised that the young ship's mate then grabbed the live shark that was as big as he was, took it under his arm and posed with it while a couple of pictures were taken. It soon started to struggle violently and the young Australian was able to hold on to it no longer. Mercifully, the shark was just as keen to get away as Zane was when he realised his error in thinking the shark was dead.

By then it was time to head on up. The journalist knew he was low on air and needing to make a shallow stop, so he picked his way back up the reef, again using his reef hook to prevent himself from bobbing buoyantly to the surface. Remember, he had no weights. Eventually, he got to the top of the reef and hooked in, extending his stop at 6 m (20 ft), the shallowest place where he could safely stay. The current was still ripping. He knew that once he was no longer tethered and had bobbed uncontrollably to the surface he would, at worst, be well on his way to the Philippines on the fast flow before the pick-up boat came back or at best, he'd need to struggle ashore somewhere and take his chances with those Komodo dragons.

He eked out the remainder of his air until his tank was empty. At this point he heard the outboard of the pick-up boat pass overhead. Surfacing, he found that Captain Matt was already in the boat and anxious to get back to the liveaboard and the therapeutic oxygen set.

He'd run out of air at depth and made a fast ascent, missing mandated deco stops. Meanwhile, there was no sign of Zane, the ship's mate.

Things were getting tense. The last time they'd seen Zane, he was cuddling a live shark. It was with great relief that he was finally spotted alive and well and floating at the surface.

"I'm sorry, guys," he reported as he climbed aboard. "At that depth and in such a strong current I was completely zonked out of my head with nitrogen narcosis."

FREE ASCENT

When things really go wrong, a novice diver discovers the only safe place to be is at the surface.

The novice diver swam calmly over to his buddy, signalling clearly that he had no air. To his horror, his buddy looked him in the eye, gave him a thumbs-up signal and dipped off the deck of the sunken freighter, down and away into the murk. A yellow fog swirled around him and debris appeared to fly by, never-endingly. He looked at the 24 m (78 ft) registering on his depth gauge and wished he'd had some better training. The locals in Java had warned him to beware of sea snakes when diving but he didn't expect his buddy to leave him for dead!

It was during the mid-eighties and he was in Indonesia on assignment to make some advertising photographs for a new airline to be called Emirates. They needed to shoot at a location called "The Thousand Islands" and they'd hired a boat that belonged to a Jakarta dive club. A couple of its members came with them, together with the advertising agency art director who claimed to be an experienced diver, and as a fledgling diver himself, with a few dives under his belt, our novice hero thought it might be a good opportunity to get a bit more time under water during any spare time that became available. He rented some diving equipment from a resort.

The oily calm surface of the water belied the powerful currents that swirled through the gaps between the islands, whipping up coral sand into no more than a metre of visibility. The local technique seemed to be to swim hard into the flow and then allow yourself to hurtle back to where you started, narrowly missing the sharp edges of giant coral heads as you went. After four dives like this our novice asked if there were any wrecks in less turbulent waters.

A day later saw them well away from the islands and moored to a topmast that was only half a metre below the surface. Relieved as he was to drop into still water, the visibility amounted to no more than a few metres. The group of four left the surface in two buddy pairs and arranged to meet on the deck of the upright wreck.

As they headed down it was noted that the paint was still undamaged on the ship, indicating it was a recent loss. Each of the Englishmen had an Indonesian buddy. Sand swirled around them as they rendezvoused on the deck, forward of the superstructure. They exchanged OK signals before heading off in separate directions. It was a large vessel but there was no idea of its displacement tonnage. Our novice diver passed over the first hold and was looking forward to his first encounter with a near-perfect ship under the sea.

It was at this moment he discovered the difference between an old-fashioned upstream regulator and a modern downstream design. The downstream design fails open and free-flows, whereas the one he had rented simply jammed shut. Of course, he didn't know this until after he had exhaled. He suddenly had no air to breathe.

He went over to his buddy but he simply gave him that fatal thumbs-up sign meaning go up, and he chased down after the others.

Next, the novice diver started to regret the rented BC. It had no independent air supply as was normal in the UK back in those days. He finned hopefully in the direction that he thought was upwards but there were no comforting bubbles to show the way. The pressure to breathe was unrelenting until kindly Uncle Boyle (Boyle's law explains that gas expands on reducing the pressure applied to it) allowed the expanding residual air in his chest to relieve that intense desire to suck in seawater.

No sooner was he comfortable than it was necessary to blow out some of this precious but now expanding air so that he didn't damage his lungs. Finning upwards as slowly as he could bear, he took care not to overtake the tiniest bubble and watched the needle of his mechanical depth gauge creep ever so slowly round its dial.

Finally, the green glow of daylight gave him cause for optimism and soon he broke the surface. He climbed back on board the boat, lay exhausted on the deck and listened as the three other divers broke the surface under the stern.

'Where's the other guy?' the art director asked.

"I don't know," the erstwhile buddy of the novice diver insisted. "He just disappeared."

The novice diver learnt several lessons that day. Make sure you can trust both your equipment and your buddy. It was his fault. He hadn't insisted on seeing any logbooks and he'd unwittingly been partnered with another novice with even fewer dives to his name than he had. He'd rented equipment that wasn't up to the job, but he'd discovered he could do a free ascent from 24 m (78 ft) deep without first taking a deep breath!

AN INTERESTING
INTERLUDE

A boat journey from a remote tropical island turns tense when the coxswain loses his way in torrential rain.

Visiting remote areas of the world is always an adventure but sometimes the adventure can be unnecessary. Kri Island is in the Dampier Strait, at the epicentre of Raja Ampat, the four island kingdoms of West Papua. The diving is spectacular with more species of coral and different fishes than anywhere else in the world, but the journey to and from the mainland can be fraught.

Tony Backhurst and his friend's transfer back from Kri Island to Sorong was by a small, but fast boat powered by two, large outboard motors. The friend had done the return journey several times before and the first time he'd departed Sorong for Kri Island he'd noticed that his coxswain had no visible means of navigation. He asked him how he knew where they were going and the man told him he took a route past the islands to his left out of Sorong and then simply kept going straight. Darkness was falling. He took the precaution of taking a bearing on his computer watch. Despite misgivings, they duly arrived at the dead of night, three hours later, at their destination. This time things were different.

It was daylight during the return leg from Kri Island but raining in such a continuous torrent that there were no visible landmarks to aid their progress. Visibility was reduced at times to only a few metres. After about two hours of motoring fast, this time the coxswain hove to and asked if either of them had a compass. He had only a school compass that was jammed with sea salt. They were slightly surprised but naturally, as divers, they were well supplied and produced a choice of three.

Tony remembered noting that the journey from Kri needed to be on a course of about 120 degrees or south east and they duly gave their coxswain the heading and helped him steer that way. From time to time through the incessant downpour they glimpsed what they thought were islands off to their starboard beam. Gradually, these became lost in the mist as it became apparent that they were being steered north east instead. They didn't know why.

Both men remonstrated with their coxswain, who would steer south east for a bit and then veer back towards the north. They were sure he was wrong but he was local, the coxswain and the expert, so they suffered an element of self-doubt. There were moments when they glimpsed some islands to the north through the non-stop downpour, and they wondered if these were the islands that should have been to their south.

They motored on for another couple of hours and then realised with dread that they were right – these islands were entirely different to those they were familiar with. They began to get cross with themselves for not having taken control of the situation earlier and the coxswain too, for obviously getting it wrong. They thundered onwards at about 20 knots burning precious petrol and going in what the Europeans were sure was the wrong direction. By now even these wrong islands had disappeared off their stern quarter in the mist of heavy rain that was still falling.

Eventually, they were down to the reserve tank of fuel and yet there was still no sign of land. Things were beginning to look very serious indeed.

At this point, Tony was able to get a signal on his iPhone and called up the GPS function. It confirmed what they had suspected. They had missed completely the vast island that makes up West Papua and Papua New Guinea and were heading out into the Pacific. They showed the position north of the land to the coxswain but, remarkably, he remained unconvinced.

At this point one of the two passengers took over the helm and steered south west. They felt like they had led a mutiny but their lives might well now be at stake. Their coxswain was still not convinced, but out of the murk appeared a primitive local fishing boat, plodding along, belching exhaust smoke, and he decided to ask them the way to Sorong.

The people on board laughed at their expense and pointed in the direction the fishing boat was going. It was south west and the direction the Europeans had been telling him since getting the GPS position. He decided to follow the fishing boat. Their own boat had a possible top speed approaching 30 knots but this fishing boat was making three knots at best. The journey became tedious but at least they were going in the right direction, provided their fuel supply held out.

It was with relief that they spotted the surf caused by waves breaking on a reef. This indicated they at last had the coast of West Papua mainland to their port side, and at this point their coxswain's confidence grew and he opened the throttles. It was with some collective relief that they headed around a final headland and saw the welcome sight of freighters at anchor outside the port, waiting to unload.

It had been an unpleasant experience that ended well, but taught the European visitors yet again, not to abdicate responsibility for their own well-being to others on the pretext that "they know what they're doing".

CURRENTS AND DRAGONS

One of the most hazardous things a diver encounters in the water is the water itself and it doesn't stay still. Then there might be dragons, too.

For 12 hours, five divers had been clinging to each other after being carried from their diving boat by the strong currents. They were British, French and Swedish. Brits Charlotte Allin and Jim Manning were experienced diving instructors working in Thailand, but they were deficient in the knowledge of local currents when they left their boat at anchor, while exploring the waters around the Komodo Marine Park, during a trip to eastern Indonesia. The diving may be spectacular, but the currents between the islands run between two of the world's biggest oceans. Not only are they strong, they are unpredictable. They should have left a capable person in charge of their boat.

Unfortunately, the extremely powerful currents they encountered denied them the chance to get back to their boat and they later found themselves drifting helplessly at the surface. Speaking to the BBC News, Jim Manning said that being in the water before landing on the island raised many concerns.

He said later that they weren't thinking about what the sharks were going to do, and stuff like that, at all. All they were worried about was the fact that they were going to be in the ocean, the waves and the wind, and if they were going to be there all night. They were going to have the sun on their faces and dehydration was going to be an important hazard. They were just worried about how they were lost at sea in a big ocean and people weren't going to be able to find them.

Presumably, nobody would have known they were missing until their unoccupied boat was discovered. After what seemed an eternity bobbing in the sea, they managed to scramble ashore on the beach of an island called Rinca, 20 miles to the south.

But severely dehydrated and exhausted, their happiness at reaching the safety of the shore was short-lived. Charlotte Allin, originally from Devon, told how that once on the beach, they spent the morning trying to make themselves visible to any would-be rescuer by building an SOS sign up on a high bank using huge white boulders. It was then that one of the other girls noticed a Komodo dragon with Jim's wetsuit in its mouth. They threw boulders at it but it wasn't scared; however, it did eventually leave the wetsuit and wander off. Komodo dragons are very efficient predators.

Dr Ian Stephen is assistant curator of reptiles and amphibians at London Zoo. He told the BBC at the time that they are potentially very dangerous animals but it helped that the divers stayed on the beach.

"Komodo dragons will eat anything that washes up on the beach. That's why these people would have been in danger. When you have animals on the brink of starvation they will be very aggressive and humans are not very powerful.

Having a couple of people throwing stones or sticks can work as long as you are only dealing with one or two. They were in danger but they did the right thing. These dragons can move incredibly quickly over short distances. The danger would have been when people started looking for food and headed inland, into long grass."

That's because a Komodo dragon's normal method of attack is to lie in ambush in long grass and then pounce on their prey. That would normally be deer, feral pigs or water buffalo. They also eat carrion.

The largest lizard in the world measuring up to 3 m (10 ft) long and 120 kg (265 lb), they are incredibly powerful. They are known to be strong surface swimmers too.

Generally, they attack their prey but don't kill it immediately. They have a toxic bite with a lethal cocktail of poisonous saliva full of different bacteria, so in a couple of days septicaemia sets in and the prey weakens and dies. A dragon can follow a blood trail for miles. They have long forked tongues with which they sense the air.

Dr Stephen told the BBC that a Komodo dragon in the wild would not hesitate to kill and eat a human if it wanted to, and although attacks on humans are rare, in 2007, an eight-year-old German boy was mauled to death.

Three of the divers were sitting together on a rock when they saw a small boat zigzagging, obviously searching for them. They were so relieved, that it was only then that they broke down and cried. They were rescued after two days of being trapped in Indonesia's tropical seas and generated a lot of interest with the British news media.

THE BFR* AND
A WATERFALL

Ocean currents are affected by underwater topography, they don't always do what you expect
them to do as three divers learnt the hard way.

"It's a BFR. The currents will be mild to wild and yes, there will
be marine life."

So went the typical dive briefing from Larry Smith, the
famous dive guide and something of a BFR himself. You can take the
man out of Texas but you can never take Texas out of the man. Larry
was a Texan, living in Indonesia. He was as wide as he was tall and
he was proud of saying, "We got things smaller round here." That was
because he'd made himself an expert on the minutiae of marine life, the
tiny and often bizarre animals that until recently had gone unnoticed
by the diving world. Some would say he'd been away from Texas too
long!

They were diving from a liveaboard called *Pelagian*, around a chain
of small islands in the eastern reaches of Indonesia, which separated the
waters of two great oceans. The dive site was to be Mark's Sharks, an

---

*A BFR is a big friggin' rock (Adjective variable)

exposed pinnacle of rock jutting up from around 60 m (195 ft) deep and defying the ocean's flow. Larry's plan was to dive at the back of this pinnacle, in the lee of the current. That wasn't good enough for three of his client divers. Matt, Mike and BJ wanted to dive the current point. That's where the current first strikes the underwater obstacle that was the pinnacle. After all, they reasoned, that would be where all the pelagic life, the big fishes, would be gathering. The current would hit the rock, split two ways and roar off. Big fishes enjoy hovering in such a flow of oxygenated water and would gather there. There's usually an eddy of water close to the rock face where three divers could stay relaxed and watch the show. Well, that's what they were expecting.

They asked if they could be dropped from the diving tender at the front of the BFR. Larry smiled benignly and acquiesced to their request. Larry made a point of giving his guests what they wanted. So three went at the front of the rock, while the others retreated in the boat to dive behind it.

As BJ descended, he witnessed something he'd never seen before. Mike had dropped a weight-pocket and it appeared to be hovering in the water, revolving slowly. Matt reached out and grabbed it, giving it back to Mike who calmly re-stowed it in his BC. It seemed surreal.

Surreal that is, until they hit the seabed. The current had been hurtling downwards with such ferocity that the three divers had involuntarily descended at the same rate as a dropped weight-pocket. That's pretty fast indeed.

The three found themselves clinging desperately to any part of the seabed they could get hold of. Rather than be pushed back out into the ocean away from the rock wall, as they feared they might, they dragged themselves to the foot of the pinnacle and set about some serious underwater rock climbing.

The water rushed forcefully over their faces, causing regulators to free-flow uncontrollably with precious air, the water and bubbles threatening to dislodge their masks. It was not pleasant. Breathing became laboured, but since it was at the beginning of the dive, they still had plenty of air supplies and they made steady progress. They had to. It was their only choice.

They determinedly inched their way upward, hands becoming torn on the sharp surfaces, fingers stung by the poisonous white hydroids that also clung to the rock surfaces and bent downwards in the flow. There was no way that they were going to release their grip on the rock and be swept back to depth. They struggled on tenaciously.

As they reached the more manageable depth of around 20 m (65 ft) deep they met another diver from their boat. He wasn't struggling at all. In fact he looked really cool and relaxed. He gazed at them with a look of incredulity, or as much incredulity that a diver can muster while wearing a mask and with a regulator stuffed in his mouth.

He assessed their predicament and kindly offered one a glove. Wait a minute! This fourth diver was hovering relaxed and calm, making no effort to swim whatsoever. Matt took the glove gratefully; slipped it on to the hand it fitted and continued his slow and arduous climb. This fourth diver ascended in an effortless controlled manner next to the three hard-working underwater rock climbers. It was again surreal. He wasn't in the flow.

Imagine an underwater waterfall. The three divers had gone down in it and were slowly climbing back up through it. The fourth diver was simply next to it. If only the three divers, fazed by the shock of their sudden descent and completely focused on climbing to safety against the downward current in the aftermath of what had been for anyone a frightening experience, had realised that before they finally made the surface.

For some reason, due to the topography of the rock (the BFR), the ocean current was hitting it and instead of being split three ways with varying degrees of intensity as might be thought normal, the full flow was being directed in a funnel downwards. It may have been unusual to be so localised but it was within this funnel of water that our three divers had inadvertently chosen to dive.

Larry Smith had sensibly taken the rest of the group into the benign conditions that surrounded it. Sadly, Larry Smith succumbed a few years later to a chest infection while in the remoter regions of Indonesia and is no longer with us, but he's not forgotten.

LOST OFF BOGNOR REGIS

Imagine floating on the surface of a glass-calm sea on a lazy summer afternoon and then imagine that you and your buddy are alone, with no sight of land, nor any boat!

The sea is a big and lonely place at times. It's dangerous, too. Tom Burton and club mate Dennis, had dropped into the water from the club's boat full of enthusiasm. The surface was slightly choppy but otherwise it was a gorgeous, English summer's day. They were about three miles offshore from Bognor in the English Channel.

Tom was relatively new to diving but Dennis, though younger, was said to be quite experienced.

A strong current was running and the two buddies were soon seen hurtling along at about 15 m (50 ft) deep, enjoying the buzz of a fast drift dive.

It was wonderful and the nearest man could get to flying like a bird. The contours of the seabed unrolled beneath them. Skates broke cover from the mud and took flight before them. Banks of dead men's fingers passed in a white blur.

Without a care in the world they stayed down for as long as the air in their tanks would let them. Then it was time to surface. The sea had taken on an oily calmness. They could see their cover boat and the tiny figures of its occupants way over on the horizon. They could make out the movements of people looking in the water.

They were obviously looking out for the divers – but in the wrong place.

Tom and Dennis shouted. They waved their arms. They whistled. They yelled. They screamed at the tops of their voices. It was all to no avail because no one looked in their direction. It was very frustrating.

And then frustration turned to disbelief. Instead of motoring over to where the divers waited, the occupants of the boat seemed to give up and headed off in the direction of Bognor. Tom looked at Dennis. Dennis looked extremely worried. They were all alone in the ocean. They could not see the low-lying coast, only endless water.

Tom told Dennis that a helicopter was bound to come to rescue them. He knew it would be all right, and he had never had a ride in a helicopter. Dennis was near to tears. Tom tried to sound calm and confident. "Maybe they'll send an RAF Shackleton to pick us up," he suggested naively.

They were wearing wetsuits. They decided to dispense with all the diving gear that was not required for their survival. They needed only their masks and fins.

Dennis dropped everything but Tom decided to keep hold of his regulator. It was the only part of his diving gear that did not belong to the club. He had only just purchased it and it was his first regulator, a Silver Snark II.

Suddenly, they became aware of an SAR helicopter. It was like a tiny yellow wasp up in the clear, blue sky and was obviously searching for them.

Again they waved as hard as they could. But the chopper turned and flew away.

Even Tom began to get depressed. He could not believe what was happening. The awful reality had dawned that they were divers lost at sea.

Tom told Dennis he was sure that nothing bad was going to happen to them. He owed someone some money and he never got away with leaving a bad debt. Tom talked about anything he could think of. Otherwise they just dozed in the water.

About six hours had passed since they had surfaced. It was an awfully long time. The sun was beginning to get low on the horizon.

Then they saw a lifeboat moving slowly in the distance. They waved furiously. Tom thought, "beautiful!" And then it too went off the other way.

Doing nothing began to play on their minds, so they decided to try to swim for the shore. The problem was that because the coast was so low-lying near Bognor they could not see which way to go.

The summer evening sun gave them a bit of a clue. They did not get very far, but it kept them busy.

Tom swam on his back. He says that he knew Dennis was spooked because he was making a definite effort to swim, whereas Tom was merely marking time. By then they had stopped talking altogether.

Tom was just dozing on his back when Dennis saw the lifeboat again. This time it was coming near. Dennis swam frantically towards it. Tom waited for it to come to him.

The lifeboat had a large net hung over the side. The two divers were grateful to be able to scramble up it.

They were soon on board and talking nineteen to the dozen. They each had a cup of tea. Tom smoked five cigarettes in succession, which was strange because he did not smoke, never had done and didn't ever!

They were asked many questions. An elderly lifeboat man had spotted them. He said everyone on board had thought they were two cormorants, but had never seen cormorants with what looked like four wings, so they had come over to have a look.

Tom and Dennis were returned safely to shore, where the press awaited them.

Tom returned home later than his wife expected. He got into bed and decided to eat the sandwiches that he had left in his car. His wife woke up and asked him if he'd had a nice day's diving, and why he had not eaten his sandwiches at lunchtime. In fact she had heard Tom and Dennis had been lost on the radio news. "She's tricky like that," Tom claimed later.

When Tom was asked what were the lessons he had learned from that experience so early in his diving career, he answered, "It seems funny to look back on now, but it certainly wasn't funny at the time. It was summer and our wetsuits were adequate, but we were lucky to be alive. We never bothered with surface marker buoys in those days. We didn't really know what they were."

"How did the boat usually find you after a dive?" he was asked. "I don't really know, but they always seemed to manage it. Diving was not organised the way it is now. We really didn't know about a lot of the dangers.

I was new to diving then and I was diving with people I thought were pretty experienced. I thought they knew what they were doing. I learned some tough lessons in those early days."

What was the single most important thing he learned from that experience?

"Always to use a marker buoy when there are tides and currents," said Tom.

ROGUE RIB

Worse things happen at sea and two divers travelling by boat encounter one of them.

The Mediterranean was dead calm. It was a Saturday morning and the channel between the island of Dragonera and the seaside village of San Telmo (now called Sant Elm) was dotted with the boats of optimistic fishermen.

The day had begun routinely – one of many during a long hot summer that a British diving instructor was spending in Majorca, teaching diving and supervising outings to local dive sites. He had set out with Caroline, a trainee, to do a straightforward safety and rescue skills test, the site for which was a sheltered and shallow bay a quick RIB ride away. A RIB is a fast open boat with inflatable sponsons that make it virtually unsinkable. It makes an ideal dive boat for short journeys to dive sites.

But things were about to go seriously wrong. By the end of the day he would be faced with the prospect of one boat cut in two, another boat out of action and a friend in hospital.

In the flat sea conditions, he was able to open the throttle right up and, with the big outboard trimmed up so that there was little area of the hull in contact with the water, they were soon skimming along at more than 35 knots.

Caroline made herself comfortable behind him on the long centre seat of the forward console, holding on to the backrest for support as they powered across the blue water in the sunshine. She recollected waving to friends out enjoying themselves in other boats as they sped past them at a polite distance. Then, without warning, something happened.

Suddenly, the boat's steering became lifeless and, before they had time to take stock of what was happening, the vessel assumed a will of its own. It veered sharply to starboard leaving Caroline and her instructor to carry on forwards at their attained speed, walking on the water for a moment.

The next moment they were swimming for their lives. Unable to counter the irresistible and totally unexpected force that had taken hold of their boat, they had been flung forwards into the water. At the speed at which they had been travelling, it was like hitting a sheet of steel.

Worse still, they then had their out-of-control RIB for company. Unmanned but with the engine still running at full throttle, the boat was hurtling round in tight circles next to them at an incredible speed – and threatening to kill them. Like some ferocious beast that had been injured, with the outboard skewed into its extreme position at one side, the boat was powering in a frantic series of tight but varying circles, its nose as the central point and its fearsomely screaming propeller at the circumference.

They had to get out of the way of that boat and out of the water fast.

Fortunately, there was help at hand. Making progress through the water as best they could in their shocked and bruised state, they managed to swim far enough away from the rogue RIB for other vessels to approach them and they were dragged from the sea to safety into a passing yacht.

But what of the RIB?

They now realised what must have happened. The steering cable must have parted somewhere along its length and the torque of the fast spinning propeller had caused the single engine to swing violently to one side, depositing the two of them into the water, while the emergency engine cut-out lead had been caught and ripped away from the instructor's shorts where it had been clipped, when he fell from the boat.

Now from safety they watched in horror as the rogue vessel continued on its erratic and menacing course. It was still hurtling round in circles like a crazy marine Catherine wheel, and they knew that with its recently filled fuel tank, it could keep going like that for three more hours.

At best it might be wrecked on the rocks or maybe collide with another boat, but there was a possibility they hardly dared consider. It appeared that it was gradually making its way towards a crowded holiday beach. It had to be stopped.

The first thought was to get close enough in another boat to throw a floating line across its path and thus tangle and ensnare the propeller, stalling the engine. Alas, they could find no boat owner prepared to get close enough.

Then they had another idea. If one of them could get close enough, maybe he could fling himself into it as it passed and cut the engine. It was a desperate plan.

The instructor persuaded some friends to lend him their small 3-metre long inflatable with its 6 hp engine, and at the last moment, Miguel, a local fisherman, offered to accompany him on his mission.

Miguel took the helm and they motored out into the channel to get close to the rogue RIB. Somehow, they had to get inside the circle being carved by it in the foaming water. The diving instructor directed Miguel to drive the little inflatable across the slower moving bow so that he could throw himself across without getting close to the fast-moving propeller at the stern.

He was focused on that high prow as the moment came and he went for it. However, at that very same moment Miguel somehow lost his nerve and cut the little outboard, bringing their little boat to a halt. As the instructor landed in the RIB he saw its propeller slice through the boards of the inflatable like a knife through butter and cut the smaller boat clean in two. Miguel was standing in the fast-sinking rear half, completely mesmerised. Then he disappeared beneath the surface. It was at this point it was realised he couldn't swim.

The instructor grabbed the engine cut-out lead and brought the roaring monster to a halt before throwing himself back into the water to swim to Miguel, who by now, was some distance from him. Only the front section of the little inflatable remained afloat and some friends in a motor yacht that had been standing by approached and he was able to see a spluttering Miguel safely dragged aboard.

Spanish pride being what it is, Miguel insisted that the RIB had struck him rather than admit he couldn't swim. Back at shore, an ambulance arrived and took him off to a trauma ward of the Palma hospital. He was out next morning unscathed, while the hapless diving instructor was off looking to buy a replacement inflatable with outboard motor for his friends, and a new steering cable for his RIB. From then on he always attached the emergency cut-out lanyard securely to his wrist.

STUCK BY STARLIGHT

Misplaced confidence can lead to fatal mistakes
as one lucky diving instructor nearly discovered.

A shore-based safari in the Sinai in the 1980s and a group of trainees on a BSAC Sports Diver course. It was a hard week, especially for the instructors. The students had extended their vocabularies, not necessarily for the better, as well as their diving skills.

The coast of the Sinai is now crowded with hotels and resorts but at that time it was a wild and lonely place. They were sleeping each night at the "Million Stars" hotel. That is to say, they searched every evening for a fairly level area of sand devoid of rocks and laid their sleeping bags there. Those without woolly hats regretted the chill of the cold desert night air.

It was an adventure. Not in the middle-of-nowhere, it was the end-of-nowhere, its farthest reach. They travelled with the Bedouin helpers in ancient Landcruisers, setting up a makeshift camp by night and diving by day. During this time, the group had improved their diving skills under the auspices of the three instructors. By the end of the week they were now certified BSAC Sports Divers.

Most had opted at the end of the course for a few celebratory beers and a barbecue. Two of the fledgling divers wanted to make one last dive at night, by underwater lamplight. An instructor escorted them.

This last and final dive of the week was to be from a site called The Tower. They'd been there before in daylight. Eschewing the water on the reef top that was too shallow to swim through yet difficult to walk across, they'd found a chimney that led down into a shallow coral cave and directly out on to the reef wall. This was to be the third dive of the day and their instructor had set a safe depth limit of only 9 m (30 ft).

Night diving is an acquired skill. A lamp will light things up in the natural colours that are denied during the daytime since everything is flooded with blue light from the daylight above. On the other hand, at night, one only sees what is lit up in the beam of the torch and there can be some loss of spatial awareness. Divers also have to be careful not to dazzle other divers with their lamps. At night, on a wall dive, there is the constant risk of dropping deeper than you intended. Depth gauges become frequently referred to.

All these things considered, after they spent a worthwhile hour enjoying the nocturnal animals going about their business in their night clothes so to speak, their instructor led them safely back into the cave.

Cautiously checking with his torch for any of the ubiquitous lionfish and other lurking poisonous spines such as those of pincushion urchins, he made his way back through the cave to the chimney.

With the lamp switched off, he could see the stars up through it, rather like looking up through a manhole. He carefully disposed of the few sea urchins loitering at the rim, in case they punctured anyone's diving suit, and drifted up.

Crunch!

The hole was too small. He was in the wrong cave! He struggled backwards down into the main cavern. There were dozens of narrow tunnels leading back from it. He wasn't sure which of them he had come along. The beam of his lamp shone on water thick and brown with stirred-up silt. Where were his trainees? They were not immediately behind him. He couldn't make out any light from their lamps.

He knew of only one certain way out. His students were still in the cave. They were probably very anxious. He knew he was. Their remaining reserves of air would not last them very long. It was very dark. Without lamps there was no light at all in the cave.

The stars glinted mockingly at him above the hole. He could reach up with his hand and feel fresh air at the surface. He started to move very fast.

His tank came off and went through first.

Crunch! went his weightbelt as he jammed even more solidly than before. Even the most super-cool among us has a panic threshold, and his anxiety was beginning to affect his judgement. He reached down to release the weightbelt but hesitated. He would need it to swim back down to the cave mouth to his trapped students, so he passed it out on to the reef top.

Wrenching himself free, his right hand smashed down between lead and rock as he forced his way through that small hole. He shouted for help from the rest of his party who were lit by firelight, busy enjoying those few beers and the barbecue far off on the beach. Nobody noticed him in the darkness, nor could they hear his shouts. The only option seemed to be to get back over the reef, find the cave and search for his newly certified divers from that end.

He turned in desperation to head back out, stumbling across the shallow reef top and was just in time to see the green glow of the torches of the other two divers rising up through the shallow water over the reef edge.

"Did you know that wasn't the right cave?" asked one.

"That's why we didn't follow you in," offered the other.

The instructor, who prefers to remain anonymous, told them that the training from the previous week had produced divers that could think for themselves. They'd passed his final test. After six weeks, his crushed hand was finally better too!

PART SEVEN

Shark Infested Waters

NICK'S BEST DIVE

A big man enters a tight cave and is relieved to get out only to find things might not be better, though it probably becomes his best dive ever!

Nick Thompson is an Australian now based in Spain. He's an amiable giant and reminds everyone of a famous film star. His friends call him Shrek. He recalled his best ever dive as one that he'd made outside a sleepy little village called Forster in New South Wales, back in his home country.

"Although all the local dive guides looked like long haired hippies, boy did they know their way around the dive sites."

He told how he once dropped off the boat and followed a couple of these "skinny fish" into a cave that was completely dark.

Switching on his lamp he thought to himself that this was not so much a cave, it was more of a tunnel about the same size that Steve McQueen and Charles Bronson might have crawled through in *The Great Escape*.

His heart rate increased as his mind filled with trepidation. Before he knew it, the shadows being cast off the walls started to make him wish he had followed the advice to use the toilet before starting the dive.

Then something bumped into him in the dark and that was it. The floodgates opened, but it was nothing to be alarmed about. It was only a grouper the size of a VW minibus that had come to see what had disturbed it from its slumbers.

Finally, the tunnel opened up wide enough to turn into a cave proper. It became big enough for this colossus of a man to turn around to see if his wife was still following behind him or "had been taken by a mythical serpent that takes great enjoyment in leaving a man without any way of feeding himself," as he put it.

She was still there and they held hands to confirm their love, or more likely it was so that they could help each other to stop shaking with fright!

Finally, the light at the end of the tunnel got bigger and the ambient light got brighter. Their nerves started to calm down and their breathing slowly returned to normal. Nick looked at his watch and was amazed at how long they had actually been under water. It was not very long at all but he saw from his tank contents gauge he had consumed a lot of air. A quickening heart and the resulting breathlessness increase air consumption dramatically.

Once illuminated by the blue window of daylight from the cave's end, they began to feel that the daunting part of the dive was over and done with. They made their way out on to the reef.

One of the hippie guides came to them and signalled a question that asked if they were all right. Of course, Nick confirmed that he was because the last thing he wanted in the world right then was to have a man who looked like he was made out of matchsticks thinking he was soft. The guide gave him a knowing wink that Nick preferred to think of as a sign of respect but it was the hippie guide's way of giving him a false sense of security. The fun part of the dive was about to begin.

The two of them were still smiling to themselves, thinking all was going to be fine, but, like the double ending to a horror movie, they turned around the corner of the reef and were confronted but at least 40 sharks.

These weren't little reef sharks. These sharks appeared to be the type that liked to eat the flesh of mammals. Not really known for taking humans but graded among the top five most dangerous sharks in Australia, these were bronze whalers, and they looked hungry.

Nick thought, "man-eaters!"

They were all facing towards Nick and his wife. This is because they were facing into the current. The divers were drifting in the current and helplessly sailing towards them. (Sharks face into the current so the oxygenated water passes through their gills and they don't have to make forward motion of their own.)

Imagine their predicament. Here they were, being propelled towards the hungry-looking sharks at a rate of knots and Nick was in a wetsuit full of what an Australian would call "nerve juice".

"Mmm," thought Nick. He was sure that he read somewhere that sharks were attracted by this and could pick up the scent. He also remembered reading in some authoritative book that sharks could sense fear.

"We felt like human pin balls bumping off these man-eaters," Nick remembered later.

It was at this point he realised why all the guides were so skinny. All the fat ones had been eaten! Nick was 130 kg (285 lb) and he felt he represented a veritable feast. He feared he was seriously starting to irritate the sharks. They probably weren't happy with the fact that he was unwillingly and repeatedly crashing into them, disturbing their chill-out time.

"Dory made it through the jellyfish in *Finding Nemo* so we can do it," he told himself.

Then something in his peripheral vision caught his attention. It was his wife and she was finning past him, head down and kicking like a mule. She was getting out of there. They passed quickly through the pack of hungry wolves and looked at where they'd been.

"Lo and behold, they'd all turned and were now facing us again. Were they in a vortex or were these guys in the grey suits ready to attack?"

It was straight back to the boat but the fellow on board looking after it was relaxing and having a beer, as Australians do. He really was not paying attention to their needs. They urgently wanted to get out of the water. They shouted to him as politely as they could to lower the ladder but, in an Australian accent, he observed laconically, "Ladder's broke, mate. You'll have to get your kit off in the water and pass it up."

Their anxiety was beginning to show but the boatman still looked unconcerned. By now his wife was out but Nick was still in the water and starting to pray. The head of one of the skinny dive guides appeared over the side of the boat, grinning at him from above. Nick wondered for a moment how he managed to get up there so quickly.

The skinny hippie told him the ladder on the other side of the boat worked perfectly.

Back on board and stowing his kit, Nick turned to one of the dive guides and asked, "What was all that about?"

"City folk – we like to wind you up a bit," was the glib reply.

"Thanks, mate, but I felt like shark bait out there."

Matchstick man shrugged his shoulders casually.

"No, mate. These sharks only feed at night. In the daytime they're really docile and almost in a state of torpidity. They won't hurt you. We dive here every day and nothing has ever happened."

Nick is still not sure whether it was his best dive or his worst.

DIVING WITH SOME BITE

Hand feeding sharks can be risky but not as dangerous as eating a reef fish.

"There was a standing wave in the Tiputa Pass in Rangiroa when we were there. The current was so strong we couldn't dive."

"There was a standing wave in the Tiputa Pass in Rangiroa when we dived it. The current was so strong, it was awesome. We saw masses of grey reef sharks and turtles, schools of huge barracuda, a couple of silver-tip sharks and finally we saw several dolphins surfing close above us while we did our safety stop."

These are two very different impressions of the same place. Divers who want to get the most out of the diving in the Tuamotus must learn how to fly the passes.

A group of low-lying atolls that form part of French Polynesia, "motu" means small island in the local languages. Don't look for them on a flat atlas. They're in that part of the world that is often omitted from an atlas due to an expedient use of space. Rangiroa is the largest of the atolls, with the world's second largest lagoon. Only Kwajalein in the Marshall Islands has larger. Rangiroa is about an hour by plane from Tahiti in the nearby Society Islands.

So why do divers go all the way there? Because in the passes of the Tuamotus they will see hundreds of sharks and there are veritable walls of them.

It's funny to read postings on the Internet by those travelling by sailboat in this area. They write things like, "We couldn't swim here because there were so many sharks," or "We managed to get back into the dinghy just before a great big shark attacked us!"

In reality it's very hard to get close to the sharks, unless there's something in it for them. Two French dive guides, Sebastian and Bertran, are the Dream Team because as far as attracting sharks goes, they rock.

No chainmail suits, no gloves, they make a habit of taking a severed Mahimahi head under their arm when they go under water and cut off pieces of the dead fish to offer individually to passing sharks.

As Canadian fellow crewmember Mike Veitch wryly observed, "We let the Frenchies do the feeding."

The Tuamotus have few passes out from of the lagoons, often only one, so when all this water flows, it flows in a torrent. Five knots is fairly normal. Ten is possible. This is a flow that can almost rip a diver's computer off his arm!

When water flows out of the atoll it takes nutrient-rich water with it, but the visibility in the pass can be very poor and if you dive it you can be tumbled out into the open ocean and be very difficult to find later. When the tide turns and the water becomes slack, the dives are very dull. There appears to be little wildlife to look at.

When the tide rises and clear ocean water floods into the lagoon, the big animals turn out to enjoy it. When divers come up after a dive they are at the surface in the restricted waters of the lagoon. They are relatively easy to find, even though the water can be exceedingly rough. A surface marker-flag proves useful more often than not.

The sharks enjoy the passes, but why? There is food in the form of prey fish and strong currents that allow them to cruise effortlessly. Otherwise they have to keep on swimming to force oxygenated water past their gills.

Neither are the grey reef sharks the top of the food chain here. A huge tiger shark and an equally impressive great hammerhead shark prey in turn on the smaller sharks. It's a shark-eat-shark world.

Sebastian and Bertran put on a good show with pieces of dead fish, even though they appear to get a few close calls with these ravenous raiders.

Isn't it a bit risky? Such an enquiry is dismissed with a Gallic shrug of the shoulders.

Bertran feeds the grey reef sharks. The sharks seem very well ordered. That is until they spot some unlucky prey near the surface. They don't mess around and a hundred or so sharks hurtle towards it in an instant. The divers never get to know what it was. All divers' cameras are pointed at Bertran, but in a moment Bertran is no longer there. He simply disappears. What the other divers are unaware of is that he has sustained a bad shark bite to his hand. It happened so quickly nobody else sees it.

He left them to instantly get washed down by the strong current through the wall of waiting sharks. He made it to the surface, was missed by the crew in the skiff and swam, all the time bleeding heavily, more than a mile back to the *Tahiti Aggressor*, their mother ship, waiting in the lagoon. That was unwise. He was bleeding so badly he might have fainted, yet the adrenalin kept him going.

The other divers don't know that at the time. They suffer a low point when he does not get back on the skiff with the rest of them after the dive. They start searching for him without luck in the white water at the surface. He's missing.

They were relieved to find him back onboard receiving first aid. He needed 20 stitches back in Rangiroa, but meanwhile another drama was unfolding. One of the Polynesian crew had been fishing, caught a reef fish and cooked and ate it in private all by himself. He not only caught a fish. He caught ciguatera poisoning too.

Eating certain reef fishes causes it. The toxin is carried up through the food chain accumulating in the larger predators such as barracuda or snappers. Ciguatoxin is very heat resistant and cannot be destroyed by conventional cooking. It's a life-threatening condition. The man became desperately ill and had to be airlifted to Papiete in Tahiti. There is no effective treatment or antidote for ciguatera poisoning, just supportive care in hospital. It seems that out in this part of the world, it's often more dangerous to bite some fishes than it is to be bitten by one.

BITTEN BY SHARKS

Chainmail suits, gloves and helmets notwithstanding, shark feeders in the Bahamas can still
get hurt.

S hark feeding is not without its risks despite the precautions taken.
In the Bahamas, the feeder nowadays wears a chainmail suit,
gloves and a football helmet. Australian Valerie Taylor, veteran
shark naturalist with her film-making husband Ron, first experimented
with chainmail suits. There was one famous television sequence where
Valerie encouraged a large shark to bite her arm. It doesn't stop you
from getting hurt though.

Leon Joubert, a one-time shark feeder in the Bahamas, experienced
a shark getting its teeth tangled in the chainmail material cladding his
arm. He wasn't bitten but in its violent struggle to get away the animal
twisted and fought and managed to break seven bones in Leon's hand,
arm and shoulder. Two nerves were severed. After a couple of lengthy
operations and nearly a year of therapy he recovered a high proportion
of the use of that arm. He later went back home to South Africa to start
a business called Bitten by Sharks.

They didn't always wear a full suit and helmet to feed sharks either.
Michelle Cove, another pioneer of shark feeding, got scalped by a shark
when she dived into an accidentally upturned bait box during a staged

feed and sustained an accidental shark bite to the back of her head. Her injury was so severe, and she was bleeding so profusely, the captain of her boat fainted when she climbed back on board.

You can pooh-pooh it but every day, long lines of people of whom few are accomplished divers, wait patiently, signed disclaimers in hand, to rent a wetsuit and a set of diving equipment in order to join a shark dive at South Ocean near Nassau. With fast boats that can carry up to 15 divers each, some days as many as 45 people get in the water each day with the same number of large hungry sharks and live to tell the tale – and what a tale it is.

Back in America where most of them hail from, they'll be regaling their disbelieving friends and neighbours with the story of how they swam with sharks and they'll have the still photographs or the video to back them up.

You can dismiss it as a circus or an underwater theatre but I'm sure that the sharks are unaware of that. They are simply there for a free handout of food. Why else would sharks want to come up from the depths to be close to noisy, air bubbling divers?

Many of these people are enjoying a day away from their cruise liner and instead of gawping at the fishes in the Atlantis Hotel's aquarium on Paradise Island, one of 51 flavours of ice cream contributing to their already super-sized girth, they get in the water and let the fish gawp at them instead. Good for them! It's good for the sharks too because when it comes to conservation, the almighty dollar takes precedence and these sharks earn a fortune for the Bahamas economy and that is why they haven't been killed, cut up and dragged off to the Far East. Shark tourism draws an estimated $78 million annual income for the national economy, and reef sharks are estimated to be worth around $250 000 each in shark tourism and shark-related activities.

The punters are usually arranged in a kneeling formation on the seabed, told to keep their arms folded and not make any sudden movements. This is to discourage them from shoving a hand unexpectedly into a passing shark's mouth. They are encouraged to use the viewfinder of their compact camera if they want to take pictures, rather than thrust the thing out in front of them in an inviting way as they look at the LCD screen. The shark feeder comes down from the boat with the bait box when everybody is ready and inevitably brings the sharks with him.

It's a fact that most of these participating guest divers don't know the difference between a regulator and the corrugated hose of their rented BC before they get in the water, but why would any experienced diver want to join in one of these shark dives?

Sharks are impressive creatures and female Caribbean reef sharks are the ones you always see in movies featuring "shark-infested waters".

Contrary to popular belief, there is no feeding frenzy. Sharks are long-lived creatures that spend their time trying not to get damaged by either their prey or other sharks. Up to 40 sharks swim round in some semblance of order and there is only a moment of urgency when one of them manages to procure a mouthful of bait and swims off in a hurry so that there is no requirement to share it.

Naturally, the people in control of the box of dead fish cuts tend to be the focus of this concentric activity. Although the hub of the feed is where the most action is, as two or three sharks compete for that final lunge, the sharks passing in and out of the circle give the keen photographer ample chance to get those natural-looking shots of sharks that are so elusive out on the reef. The first rule of good quality underwater photography is to get close, then get closer still. These sharks come very close. They often come close enough to touch, and touch you they often do as they swirl by. You can even see the tiny "ampules of Lorenzi", which are the pressure-sensing nerve endings around the sharp end of the animal, as it passes.

An enlightened Bahamian government has encouraged the dive centre to sink as many wrecks as possible in shallow water for the benefit of divers. Some of these wrecks are covered in coral growth while others remain strangely bare.

The young people that take on the job of shark feeding are very competitive. They certainly like to try to outdo each other. Chang, a Chinese Australian and one of the most experienced feeders, has taken to feeding the sharks around the aft deck of one of the intentionally sunk-for-divers wrecks; one without any coral growth to speak of.

He likes to have the audience holding safely on to the outside of the stern railings with the chainmail-clad company photographer and the videographer waiting ready so that he can arrive theatrically on the upper part of the superstructure surrounded by the sharks. They look almost like a bunch of very overweight pigeons as they circle around him. Then he can leap, weightless and super-hero-like, down on to the deck and start the feed.

It gives an interesting background to the photographs and while Chang the chainmail-clad feeder is doing his stuff for the benefit of the paying audience, the underwater photographer can also get unusual shots of sharks swimming round the rusting metal.

Of the thousands of paying guests who enjoy these shark-feeding experiences, none have ever been injured by the sharks. However, it's always on the cards for those holding the bait. That's because a shark closes its eyes with a special nictitating eyelid at the final moment when it grabs the bait and mistakes can be made by both shark and feeder. Watching divers never feel threatened. The sharks are focused on the cuts of dead fish offered.

It's not something you see every day but you can be sure the feeder keeps his hands away from those hungry mouths, chainmail or not.

FACE OFF A TIGER

When it comes to feeding, there's a strict hierarchy in the shark world because size matters.

Mike Neuman was a successful Swiss banker and his passion was scuba diving. When he retired, he moved to the South Pacific and invested some of his hard-earned fortune in a small dive centre in the Fiji islands, at Beqa Lagoon.

James Beazely had been a gentleman's gentleman, a butler. That's probably how he met Mike. He was almost archetypical; English, beautifully well spoken, a civilised man and not the sort of person anyone would expect to be working with a highly frenetic shark feed, possibly famed as the world's best, with as many as eight different species of shark turning up for a handout of food. James became the unlikely managing director of Beqa Adventure Divers.

Sharks eat fish, and they are especially good at clearing up the remains of dead fish. It's amazing that in the chaos of bouillabaisse that happens when lots of bait and fish blood is released into the water, the sharks don't accidentally bite each other, but strict rules apply in this world. Among sharks, size matters.

Sharks boost adrenalin levels among divers. The first shark that recently certified divers are thrilled and likely to see early in their tropical diving outings, is the little white-tip reef shark.

As a species, it's a voracious nocturnal hunter but it spends many of its daylight hours resting on a sandy patch of seabed, pumping water through its gill slits. This rubbery species can grow impressively big, yet there is always that nagging feeling that a white-tip reef shark is merely a big dogfish with ideas above its station. Not so the little black-tip reef shark.

This can be encountered nervously speeding about in the shallow water of the reef top. It's a pretty, two-toned job, has the proportions of a real shark and can look impressive in photographs, where the casual observer cannot tell that this species is rarely more than a metre long. Black-tips and white-tips both defer to the larger, grey reef shark.

This is a proper shark, the type you see in movies. Take a photo home of yourself with one of these and you will certainly impress your non-diving neighbours.

Grey reef sharks tend to patrol the fringes of the reef where it meets deeper water. They are quick and perpetually looking for the next meal. Grey reef sharks defer to larger lemon sharks.

Lemon sharks are elegant-looking creatures. It's nice to see one cruising around, escorted by a bundle of little pilotfish keeping station at its nose and anticipating its every change in direction. Lemon sharks have two dorsal fins of almost equal size, and a long slim body. Lemon sharks seem unaggressive and defer to tawny nurse sharks when half-heartedly competing for food.

Tawny nurse sharks don't mess about when it comes to eating. They are large sharks with small mouths. They can suck their prey right out from under a rock and could suck the flesh off the thigh of any diver that bugs them.

Nurse sharks lie about on the seabed, usually safely under overhangs, when they are not actively hunting, which they do at night. They are powerful. Divers who have watched several full-grown specimens skirmish over a meal, suggest it's best to keep your distance.

They prefer not to swim in open water, and stay close to the substrate. During squabbles, their long tail fins churn the seabed up, soon reducing the visibility to a murkiness that can lead to the accidents that happen when other sharks can't see what they're doing. If an encounter with any of these sharks has put the wind up you, you haven't seen a big shark!

Tawny nurse sharks defer to bull sharks. Bull sharks prefer murky conditions and have poor eyesight. They have been implicated in plenty of attacks on swimmers, though these were probably all accidents.

You might think these large sharks are ordinarily timid, despite their massive girth and equally wide maw. They look very scary, but in fact keep their distance unless there is food in the water and the visibility has been reduced, say by a couple of squabbling nurse sharks.

It's then that bull sharks become bold. A large bold predator like this can be impressive, especially once you've noted its tiny piggy eyes and realised that it is probably not very good at grabbing precisely what it was aiming for. It just opens its terrifying mouth, closes its eyes and goes for it. Bull sharks start by circling in pairs. It's all very leisurely at first, but gradually they get confident and the carousel begins to speed up.

Once a diver is surrounded by half a dozen or more competing bull sharks and things are getting a little frenzied, he starts to ignore what the other fish are doing. These are the sharks of nightmares, a cross between Jaws and Mr Magoo. They add a distinct edge to any fish feed.

Big, grey and purposeful, they need a large amount of food every day and are determined to get it. The sumo wrestlers of the shark world, even a bull only 3 m (10 ft) long is a very heavy animal.

But bull sharks soon get forgotten when the tiger shark arrives. Bull sharks defer to tigers. In fact, while the tiger is there, they make themselves scarce. Tigers defy description.

Look out of your window at passing cars. If a grey reef shark is a Ford Focus and a bull shark a Mercedes limousine, the tiger shark is a cross between a Hummer and a JCB. Any of them can kill you if it hits you, but if it's the tiger shark, no one will bury your remains. There will be precious little left as evidence that you ever existed.

The tiger shark arrives wraith-like. Suddenly it's there and nothing else seems to matter. This particular tiger shark is 6 m (nearly 20 ft) long, and that's a lot of shark! It has distinctive stripes on its flanks even though textbooks say that the stripes disappear with adulthood.

Tiger sharks are the garbage men of the ocean. The stomachs of caught specimens have revealed all sorts of paraphernalia, including car tyres and tin cans. A tiger shark is as likely to gobble up a diver's camera rig if offered, on the off-chance that it might taste good. And do you know what? You'd let it!

One particular visitor to Beqa Lagoon has two or three large hooks festering in the corner of her mouth, presumably left there by some fishermen who'd gone home to get a bigger boat.

Scarface, as she is named, is a regular at the shark feeds and when she turns up, all the other sharks remember urgent things they should be doing elsewhere. Tiger sharks are partial to dining on smaller sharks, especially little black-tips and grey reefs. Scarface is unstoppable. Shark enthusiast Mike has made lots of close-up portraits of Scarface with his camera. His managing director James Beazeley often went on Beqa shark-feed dives too, but when one day Scarface pinned him helplessly against the reef wall, he decided to give up diving and go back to being a butler.

TONIC IMMOBILITY

It seems to be well known that if you take a shark by the tail and dorsal fin and turn it on to its back, it becomes torpid and in a state of tonic immobility.

Shark feeders the world over, clad in their chainmail suits, are happy to demonstrate tonic immobility during staged feeds, grabbing and turning a shark passively on to its back and impressing their human diving audiences no end.

It was probably the young Stuart Cove, living and diving with his friends in the Bahamas, who first discovered this phenomenon. But how? How do you discover that by grabbing hold of a large cartilaginous fish in this way, a fish that can double back on itself and is armed with multiple rows of razor-sharp teeth that can rip an arm off in a moment, you can send it torpid?

Stuart became famous in Hollywood as the shark wrangler to the movies. If you are a film director and you want a shark in your film, you go to Stuart Cove to fix it. He built his reputation during the filming of the James Bond film *Never Say Never Again*, an adaptation of Ian Fleming's *Thunderball*.

The production company had three tiger sharks previously caught and kept in a moon pool on a boat. The requirement was for a shark to swim through the shot so that it looked like James Bond had successfully evaded it while swimming into the wreck of *The Tears of Allah*.

The tigers had gone torpid since being kept stationary and it was the job of a group of divers to jump-start the selected shark before releasing it. They did this by pushing the animal through the water, rushing oxygenated water through its gills until it woke up and could swim off. It was then to be filmed and another group of divers had the job of catching the now wide-awake animal. This was not the best job on the set! Stuart was one of the shark catchers.

There is a Hollywood maxim that goes along the lines of "Never work with children or animals". True to form the first shark did not swim where it was expected to go and no good "take" was made. The second tiger shark was prepared and again it swam out of shot. In both cases, the foolhardy young men that had volunteered to do the catching failed in their mission. Both sharks escaped.

The production team was down to their last tiger shark. The same thing happened. The shark was jump-started and swam off in the wrong direction. Stuart surfaced to hear the director going ballistic. He decided to make himself scarce. He swam off and found one of the tigers swimming stupidly into a net and getting nowhere. Tiger sharks may be the most fearsome undersea predator but they are not known for great intellect. So he simply turned the stripy giant around and redirected it back towards the underwater movie set (by the way, you can still dive these Hollywood sets today). The shark slowly swam back and Stuart swam alongside it, arriving back to be acclaimed the top shark wrangler in the world for movies, a title that he has maintained until today.

So how did he discover tonic immobility, the ability to make a shark torpid by turning it on to its back?

I asked him and he explained in one word. "Kalik."

As a young man, he and his friends would venture out to a vast American AUTEC buoy that is tethered from time to time in the incredibly deep waters of the nearby Tongue of the Ocean. This buoy, as big as a small island, is used by the American Navy as a floating structure to haul down equipment to test for use at extreme depths. AUTEC stands for Atlantic Undersea Test and Evaluation Center.

It casts such a huge shadow, all manner of pelagic fish gather in schools beneath it. This includes the fast growing and immensely tasty Dorado or Mahimahi and silky sharks. The boys would head out there to fish for Mahimahi and while cleaning their catch, the silky sharks would gather in droves around their boat to feast on the fish cleanings. The foaming surface would seethe with their grey bodies.

The other thing associated with fishing is beer. Kalik is the local Bahamian beer. They'd always take a case or two with them, and emboldened by alcohol it was inevitable that at some point, one lad would bet another that he wouldn't dare get in the water with the feeding silky sharks.

One thing leads to another and over time, these bets extended to swimming round the boat and eventually grabbing hold of passing sharks. Once enough Kalik had been consumed, the illusions formed by alcohol made it seem easy enough to grab hold of a shark safely, and that is how the properties of tonic immobility were discovered.

In fact, these young people went on later to scuba dive with the sharks, grabbing them, turning them, aiming them at another friend under water and releasing the shark like a missile! It seemed only a small step to offer their services as shark catchers when Hollywood came to the Bahamas. Stuart Cove became the world's top shark wrangler and today tonic immobility is widely in use as a technique for conservation work on sharks by divers as it allows the removal of fishing hooks from live animals and broken lines that they might be trailing.

PART EIGHT

Tragedies

THE TRAGIC DEATH OF
DAVID GRAVES

Tragedy strikes a promotional press trip to the
Bahamas.

The stories collected here are not just about diving to extraordinary depths, or discovering untold treasure. Divers may experience dangerous encounters with sea creatures but these are usually of their own making. These are the stories of things that have happened under water, many witnessed first-hand by the author and, as far as danger goes, exemplified by the tragic story of the last day in the life of David Graves.

David Graves was a highly experienced and respected journalist working for the *Daily Telegraph*. He had just turned 50. He had dodged bullets in Northern Ireland and had fulfilled assignments in many dangerous places round the world. As something of a thank you from his employer, he was assigned by his newspaper to cover a travel-leisure story, and joined a group of journalists from other newspapers with a view to diving the blue holes of the Bahamas in Andros.

The very word Bahamas conjures up images of luxury and piña coladas consumed while relaxing in the warm subtropical sunshine. Each of the journalists involved had grabbed the chance of what appeared to them to be an easy task. Jane Ridley wrote later in the *Guardian* newspaper that, like hundreds of journalists every year, David and the others accepted the all-expenses-paid "facility trip" in their own holiday time on the understanding they would write a travel piece.

However, blue holes are the entrances to prehistoric cave systems subject to strong tidal flows, and as such, are no place for anyone but the most experienced cave diver. None of these journalists had any more experience under water than they might have gained diving in the most benign conditions. A non-diving member of staff from the Bahamas Tourist Office in the UK escorted them on the trip.

Jeff Birch, the owner of Small Hope Bay dive centre, had years of experience dealing with expert and would-be expert divers. He quickly spotted that these people were neither experienced enough nor had any real understanding of what blue hole diving was about, and decided to take them out for a shallow checkout dive. Few of the group appeared confident in the water and it was easily apparent that plans had to be changed. Ironically, David Graves appeared to be one of the most confident of the group while under water, up until he suddenly revealed that he had run out of air from the supply in his tank and shot to the surface.

Shooting to the surface from depth can be hazardous in itself and a more appropriate method of dealing with an ill-managed air supply would be to temporarily share the aqualung (equipped with an alternative second-stage regulator for the purpose) of another diver while ascending at a safe rate.

The problem for Jeff Birch was that he had a group of divers, all journalists, with a great opportunity to get some international publicity for diving in the Bahamas; however, the itinerary for the week's activities had to be aborted since none of them were sufficiently skilled as divers for the task originally planned. That afternoon he decided to stage a shark feed as a bit of underwater entertainment and education, in the most benign conditions he could find.

He sent the group with his two diving guides by boat to a relatively shallow spot that had gin-clear visibility under water with almost no current whatsoever. The maximum depth (18 m or 60 ft) was well within that to which the most inexperienced yet certified diver should be limited.

One of the dive guides escorted the group of journalists, plus a couple of tourist guests that were staying at Small Hope Bay Lodge, down on to the seabed where they were instructed to kneel, stay still and watch the show. It was remarked later that even though this group of divers were lacking in-water experience, some of them had chosen to take cameras with them, increasing their task loading.

A previously frozen bucketful of fish scraps was lowered into the water on a wire hawser from the surface, so that it dangled like a giant popsicle. This attracted a few Caribbean reef sharks that swam round the popsicle, biting off parts as they defrosted in the warm ocean waters. This happened in an orderly manner until the last bit of fish fell loose from the melting ice block and a few sharks tussled over ownership of it. This brief moment of frenetic energy could be described as shark rodeo.

If you've never seen a shark at close quarters before, this could be said to be quite exciting to witness, but once the bait was gone there was nothing to keep the sharks there and they were soon gone too.

The seabed at this location is virtually nothing but clear sand apart from a couple of coral heads. The dive guides led their charges slowly round these coral heads and thereafter back to the anchor line of the boat.

As mentioned before, the speed of ascent and the pressure changes encountered can be a hazardous part of the dive. It is usually recommended that a diver ascends at less than 10 m (30 ft) each minute and waits for three minutes at a depth of around 5 m (15 ft) before proceeding even more slowly to the surface. The dive guides were intent that none of their charges was going to ascend too quickly and encourage a health-threatening decompression event.

They gathered them into a group and herded them slowly up the line with one guide above and another below, until something happened to one of the divers. It is still arguable exactly what, since she did not attend the later court hearing and give evidence. She probably lost her weightbelt by accidentally unhitching it, leading to a massive increase in buoyancy. Both dive guides were involved in rectifying the situation and were distracted for that moment. One held the affected diver safely at that depth while the other went back down to retrieve the dropped weights.

At that same time, David Graves decided to leave the group and was seen by a single witness to swim off purposefully. Later examination of the images in his camera revealed he had gone back to photograph a large brain coral. Suffice to say that the group continued the ascent without the dive guides noticing he was no longer with them.

It was only moments after the rest of the group were safely back on board the boat that he was noticed missing. One of the guides immediately jumped back into the water and found him lying lifeless on the sandy seabed near the coral head, his air tank totally empty.

He was raised to the surface and his cyanosed body quickly, yet carefully, brought back on to the deck of the boat where valiant and expert efforts were made to resuscitate him by those that knew how.

Jane Ridley wrote that they watched, in horror, as he was given resuscitation. All they could do was cling to each other and pray, but "their prayers weren't answered".

David Graves did not regain consciousness and although resuscitation continued during the long journey back to an American naval base where expert medical care was available, he was declared dead on arrival. Post-mortems later confirmed, "The cause of death was acute pulmonary oedema due to drowning."

How could this terrible tragedy have happened?

A cursory browse of the recorded dive profile on his diving computer watch at this time, combined with the pictures and time code recorded by his camera, revealed a lot of what had happened.

After taking his last picture he suddenly shot directly to the surface. This would have probably coincided with him discovering his tank was finally and completely empty. The diving computer does not record the last couple of metres (6 ft) of an ascent but it might be assumed he fought his way to the surface. Weighed down with diving equipment and still wearing his weightbelt, David Graves should have blown some air by mouth into his buoyancy control device at this time. This is a routine procedure for a trained scuba diver and would have enabled him to float safely.

THE TRAGIC DEATH OF DAVID GRAVES

Why he did not, or why he did not release his weightbelt as it is designed to be jettisoned in an emergency such as this, is a mystery but it is obvious from his diving computer profile that he was unable to stay with the life-preserving fresh air.

People do not usually drown the way it's depicted by movie directors. It's usually a very quiet affair. Exhausted from swimming an impossible swim, David Graves tragically dropped and drowned, leaving behind in England a distraught widow, two young sons and a lot of angry questions.

"How can a perfectly fit and healthy man die so easily under water?" was the sort of question printed in several national newspapers at the time. The truth is, that the most hazardous thing you will meet under water, is the water itself.

BRET GILLIAM AND THE SHARK ATTACK

The oceanic white-tip shark used to be the most prolific large animal on the planet and it was known to be a man-eater.

This is not a pretty story. It happened a long time ago and it might put you off ever going in the water again. Be warned! It's the well-documented story of a shark attack that happened in 1972. Shark experts speculated at the time that the sharks might have been attracted, and then stimulated, by the low frequency sound in the water from nearby submarine testing.

Bret was always a powerfully built man and those that know him know that he has a powerful character too. A lesser man would not have survived the ordeal told here. His buddy did not.

Three divers set up a dive at Cane Bay in St Croix, US Virgin Islands. They were Rod Temple, a Brit, and two Americans, Robbie McIlvane and Bret Gilliam. Their purpose that day was to recover some samples from a collecting experiment they had placed previously on the reef wall for a local marine science lab. It was at 65 m (210 ft) deep. They also needed to shoot some pictures. It was before the advent of diving computers, so their carefully chosen plan was transferred to a diver's slate they each carried. They'd made the same or similar dives hundreds of times before.

"Two of the navy vessels that we worked with on submarine listening tests were just a few miles offshore, and we could hear their acoustical sound generators pinging away as we descended."

The work finished, Rod excitedly tapped Bret on the shoulder as two oceanic white-tip sharks swam closely by. It was unusual to see this type of shark so close to the reef. In fact it was as unusual as seeing two wildebeest grazing in Times Square.

Bret and Robbie headed back on up but became separated from Rod. Bret went back down to look for him. What Bret saw next and what then happened are described here in his own words.

"I reached Rod and things were about as bad as they could get. One of the sharks had bitten him on the left thigh without provocation and blood was gushing in green clouds from the wound. I was horrified and couldn't believe my eyes. He was desperately trying to beat the 12-foot long animal off his leg and keep from sinking deeper. I had no idea where the second shark was and lunged to grab his right shoulder harness strap to pull him up.

Almost simultaneously the second shark hit Rod in the same leg and bit him savagely. I could see Rod desperately gouging at the sharks' eyes and gills as he grimly fought to beat off his attackers. With my free hand I blindly punched at the writhing torsos of the animals as they tore great hunks of flesh from my friend in flashes of open jaws and vicious teeth. Locked in mortal combat, we both beat at the sharks in frantic panic.

We were dropping rapidly now, completely out of control. My efforts to kick up were fruitless as the sharks continued to bite and tear at their victim, all the while dragging us both deeper. I felt Rod move again to fend off another attack and my hopes soared upon realizing that he was still alive.

Both sharks retreated into the blue and I watched them circle our position from about ten feet away. To my horror I saw one shark swallow the remains of Rod's lower left leg right before my eyes. The other gulped a mouthful of flesh it had torn off.

Rod and I came face to face for the first time during the attack. He shook his head weakly and tried to push me away. I grabbed for his waist harness for a new grip and felt my hand sink into his mutilated torso. There was no harness left to reach for. He had been partially disembowelled.

Shrieking into my mouthpiece in fury, I pulled him from the coral and took off pumping for the surface with him clutched to my chest. Immediately, the sharks were on us again. I felt the larger one actually force me to one side as it savagely sought to return to the wounds that gushed billows of dark blood into the ocean around us. Rod screamed for the last time as the second shark seized him by the mid-section and shook him. The blue water turned horribly turbid with bits of human tissue and blood. Then we were turned completely over and I felt Rod being torn away from me.

I watched his lifeless body drift into the abyss with the sharks still hitting him. The attack had started around 60 m (200 ft). My depth gauge was pegged at 100 m (325 ft) but I knew we were far deeper than that."

Bret then made a remarkable free ascent from the extreme depth after his air supplies ran out. He suffered decompression illness from which he finally recovered after being evacuated to Puerto Rico by an emergency flight.

Robbie's last view of Rod and Bret was as they were dragged over the wall in a cloud of blood by the sharks. He never saw Bret's free ascent and so reported them both killed when he got to shore. It was not until Bret called his father from the hyperbaric hospital a day later that it was known he had survived. The previous depth that a diver survived a free ascent from was 55 m (180 ft). Gilliam was probably closer to 120 m (400 ft). He was cited for heroism by the US Virgin Islands government for risking his own life to try to save his partner. In 1993, the BBC produced a television special based on the incident as part of a series called *Dead Men's Tales*.

In 2010, five people were attacked while swimming in the sea at Sharm el Sheikh in Egypt. Four were horribly maimed and one was killed. It is thought that an oceanic white-tip shark was probably responsible.

TRAPPED!

Trapped under water in a wreck with no way out must be every diver's nightmare.

James Tuttle had only recently joined the diving liveaboard *Royal Evolution*, operating between Egypt and the Sudan, as a dive guide, when he asked a passenger that had been on similar trips before, to guide him around inside the wreck of the *Umbria*, a wartime passenger liner scuttled in Port Sudan.

That passenger later wrote, "One wrong turn was all it needed. My heart started to race as I suddenly realised the implications; that my lifeless body might only be recovered long after I ran out of anything to breathe. What an awful feeling it is, when you realise you are trapped inside a wreck at night. You can get disorientated and lost so easily. Everywhere I looked, was very familiar except that it seemed that whatever direction I swam in, I was confronted by an impenetrable bulkhead. After three or four attempts at different routes and seeing even our careful finning beginning to stir up the sediment and reduce the visibility, my anger at not finding what I was looking for began to turn to fear; the fear that we might never find our way out. It was then that my heart began to climb out of my chest. My buddy James seemed oblivious to our predicament. He trusted me. I was responsible.

We've all made mistakes, but in diving, some mistakes can be fatal. I'd dived the wreck many times before, so when James asked me to show him where the three Fiat cars were stowed, I didn't hesitate. Alas, the difference was, that it was a night dive and there were no telltale patches of blue daylight to indicate the direction of the route back out. It was just a question of whether what was the rich blackness of the night was going to eventually reveal itself as another dead end, or if we'd hit the open space of the ocean. It was the beginning of the dive, we were shallow and we had masses of gas to breathe but nevertheless I was relieved to eventually find the strobe I'd previously placed at the exit to safety. Obviously one such light was not enough and an important lesson had been learned. Despite the wreck being so familiar, like Theseus of Greek mythology, we should have used a reel and line.

Once we came across a familiar pile of bottles I knew we were in the wrong hold. Gaining my bearings, I was able to get directly to the cars. This time, however, I took the precaution of not only repositioning the strobe but I left my back-up light tied off at the turning point where we lost sight of the strobe. It's not a difficult penetration but don't do it after dark!"

Barbara Wilson had a similarly frightening experience diving with her BSAC branch in the frigid waters of Scotland's Scapa Flow. It's the site of the scuttling of the German Imperial Navy in 1919 while interned, and also some naval wrecks from World War II.

These Dreadnought battleships carried heavy guns on deck, so they tended to invert as they sank and the *Kron Prinz Wilhelm* is typical. It has not been subject to much salvage. The seabed is at 38 m (125 ft), so besides being extremely cold and murky, it's also deep. In order to see any part of the wreck the diver needs to get underneath the upturned deck.

Barbara's logbook reads, "Went through a hole in the wreck and got caught up in the narrow part. I was stuck. I had to steady myself and think hard not to panic. I went through my air very quickly."

It was typical British understatement. In fact, later she reported that it had "scared her to death". She had to carefully wriggle backwards being careful not to get hooked up on any torn metal. Luckily, she moved cautiously backwards in exactly the same way as she had arrived, and after a few tense minutes managed to free herself. The problem with these deep wrecks is that it's so dark; with no visual clue as to where the surface might be, a diver might unknowingly ascend into a closed space. Luckily, she didn't.

"I didn't see much of the wreck. It was so dark. I only saw the few bits close up that were lit by my lamp."

Some divers have been less lucky.

The wreck of the *Zenobia*, a Swedish roll-on roll-off truck ferry that sank outside Larnaca harbour in 1980, after encountering troubles with its ballast tanks, has become a popular dive site; yet has claimed the lives of several divers that have dared to venture inside without proper training or the means to retrace the route.

Imagine the horror of finding yourself trapped in an air pocket behind a sealed picture window of the main saloon, as one girl diver did in the early days after people first started diving on the *Zenobia*.

Her partner and dive guide had already left her in a fatal attempt to find a route out but by this time so much debris and silt had been stirred up by their progress that underwater visibility had been reduced to nothing. She stayed where she was. Out of air from her tank but breathing from this air pocket, all she could do was signal frantically to other divers she saw passing by. Alas, they thought she was giving them a friendly wave.

Back on the dive boat, these divers compared notes about seeing this diver inside the window and their Cypriot dive guide, Paris Elftheriou, immediately deduced this was a disaster in the making. He donned his dive gear and bravely headed back down. He knew that so soon after his previous dive he risked his health but there was no option but to try to get her out. He took a lead weight and was able to use it to break the window and free her before it was too late. However, this also freed the bubble of trapped air that sustained her and they had to make a hurried ascent to the surface sharing what air he had left in his tank. Both were severely injured with decompression illness but at least they survived to tell the tale.

Ian McMurray, a chirpy Liverpudlian, runs a dive centre close by, and has since made literally thousands of dives on the wreck. Some of these have not been enjoyable. They have been the ones to find and recover the bodies of divers who lost their way inside.

On this day he arrived at the dive site in his own boat just as the disaster was unfolding. It seems that the girl was one of a group of four but two of them had by then found their way out. Ian went into the water with his assistant Niall and started to make a systematic search of the wreck for the missing buddy of the girl. The difference was that Ian was connected to a long rope that Niall fed to him from outside of the wreck. In that way Ian was unlikely to get lost.

Within the structure an underwater labyrinth consisted of more than 50 cabins leading from a series of corridors. After years in seawater, most of the wreck was in a state of collapse. The chipboard walls and ceilings were wafer-thin and disintegrated into liquid pulp at the slightest touch. The cabins were a tangled web of wires, cables and broken furniture. A thick layer of silt covered everything and was easily disturbed to reduce the visibility to zero.

Eventually, inching his way through this house of horrors, Ian came across a diver's foot barely inches from his face. It was something that a lesser man might have been freaked out by, but it was that of the man he had been looking for. It had been two hours since the casualty had gone missing and there was no hope for him but Ian was able to bring his lifeless body back to the surface. Ian McMurray later received an award for bravery from the Cypriot president for his heroic search efforts.

THE RISING TIDE

The disastrous tsunami of Boxing Day 2004 affected many people in different ways, not least those with dive centres in remote locations.

Ton and Marjan Egbers looked out to sea with a slight feeling of unease. It was the day after Christmas and their guests had gone out in the boat for an early morning dive. The Dutch couple, originally from Delft, had previously worked as dive guides in Thailand but had now settled in Pulau Weh, an island that is the most western point of Indonesia's Sumatra. This is where they set up their own dive centre in 1998.

They were attracted to the island of Pulau Weh by the clear water and the stupendous underwater topography, but not least for the fact that they could build a dive centre close to the dive sites, so that they were absolved of the logistical difficulties they had experienced in Thailand.

Gapang Beach was not a highly developed resort. A line of improvised shanty-style buildings followed the contour of the sandy beach, a few metres inshore. Locals plied a trade in basic necessities for foreign travellers.

The diving business had been difficult at first, but it slowly built up by word of mouth. It was not helped by the fact that the area was under martial law thanks to the activities of the local secessionists, but backpackers came and demand for diving courses flourished. Eventually, they had been able to move out of the temporary accommodation on the crude veranda of a Gapang Beach cafe. They had got enough money together to build an impressive two-storey concrete and brick structure that now housed their business, the Lumba Lumba dive centre. It was the only proper construction on Gapang Beach.

But this morning Ton and Marjan were anxious. They had spent the night in the classroom of the dive centre and a few earthquake tremors during the night had woken them even from their post-Christmas celebrations slumber. Now they were witnessing an abnormally low tide and were worried that their dive boat might be run aground, when it returned loaded with happily fulfilled divers.

They were standing on the road surveying the scene when Ton noticed that the tide was beginning to rise again and this time rising abnormally quickly.

They had never witnessed it rise so high. Soon it was spilling up to the edge of the track that separated the beachfront businesses from the sandy beach, and then, quite miraculously, it started to recede. They had never seen anything like it.

But it didn't just recede. It was as if some invisible force was drawing the sea away from the land. Soon the house reef was exposed to the air. Marjan remembers to this day the smell of the coral. Unease turned to alarm and they backed away to the area 50 m (164 ft) from the road where big concrete rinse tanks stood under the shade of a large corrugated iron roof. Something eerily strange was happening.

Soon the sea was back again. There was no tidal wave. The sea level simply rose and rose, unstoppably. The water poured over the roadway and pooled around the concrete piers of the dive centre. Soon it was a few feet deep. Marjan climbed on top of the rinse tanks in an effort to keep her feet dry. Ton climbed a tree nearby. Marjan's feet started to get wet and she vainly tried to climb on to the corrugated iron roof but the overhang prevented her from doing so. Ton called to her to climb across to the branches of the tree.

Eventually they found themselves floating in water and holding on to the topmost branches. The high roof of the rinse tank area by now was completely submerged.

Other guests had made their way on to higher ground behind the dive centre as the water level had risen. They called to Marjan and Ton to swim to them. By now the water was almost covering the upstairs windows of the dive centre and no other building was left visible. The water around the dive centre was by now more than 7 m (23 ft) deep. When was it going to stop?

A German girl reached down to help drag Marjan out and just as she gripped her wrists and pulled, all that water rushed away with a mighty roar. It was if someone had pulled the plug.

The water rushed away in that awful moment, taking all before it. The roughly constructed wooden buildings, the cars, the motorbikes, the contents of the dive centre, including their compressor that smashed its way through a brick partition wall, the corrugated iron roof that had shaded the rinse tanks and everything else went with it.

The people of Gapang Beach, both locals and visitors, gaped in horror as everything they possessed disappeared before their very eyes. They were left with nothing more than the clothes they stood up in. Luckily everyone was safe, even though Marjan and Ton had experienced a narrow escape.

Imagine the feelings too, of the divers in the boat, returning from a jolly morning dive. They hadn't been affected by the changing tidal height while they had been at sea. Imagine what it was like to arrive and find the beach strangely empty. No clutter of rudely constructed timber shacks that had provided their eating places and their accommodation; just the solitary shell of the concrete and brick building that had once been that proud new dive centre, remained as witness to what had happened.

Imagine too, the loss of communications. Nobody had any idea that this had not just been a local event. One British and Japanese couple from Singapore were due to fly back. They made their way across the mountainous island to the port only to find the high-speed ferry service was not operating. Ever resourceful, they hired a fishing boat to take them to Banda Aceh. They had no idea that they were heading for the epicentre of the earthquake that had caused the tsunami.

Banda Aceh is a big town that lies on a flat coastal plain. They were unaware of the horror that was about to face them when they arrived.

Here the tsunami had formed a rolling wave, sweeping all before it. Nobody in the town had any warning of their impending doom. A total of 50 000 people were drowned in their homes, their cars, in the streets and in the surrounding fields in Banda Aceh that day.

The couple made an arduous and emotional way by foot the 6 km (4 miles) to the airport, where they managed to board a military plane out of that hell-hole. Their hike involved stepping over the bodies of endless numbers of people, men, women and children, that had been drowned or crushed in the murderous tidal wave of water, smashed concrete and torn steel. The buildings of the town had simply been swept away.

The power of this tidal wave beggars belief but if you consider that an electrical power-generating station, built on a massive barge as big as a cruise liner, was swept from its moorings and carried many miles inland, crushing anything that stood before it, you get the idea. That barge is now a would-be tourist attraction, a grim reminder of the past horror, and today's visitor inevitably wonders how many people still lie beneath it.

That was December 2004 and everything has been rebuilt since the disaster happened. Banda Aceh is now again a thriving town with picturesque fishing boats in its harbour, if also filled with less than picturesque sharkfins drying in the sun. Its modern airport provides a link to the rest of the world. One house owner has turned her own disaster into a dramatic memorial. She still has a fishing boat sitting atop the place where generations of her forebears had once lived and she herself had brought up a family.

THE FATAL LURES OF DEPTH AND FAME

Attaining great depths can lure a diver to take risks with his life, as one very famous diver demonstrated and paid the price.

Cave divers used to tell a joke about some of their number who died and went to heaven. St Peter met them at the Pearly Gates and asked what they wanted to find in their perfect heaven. "A wonderful cave system that no one had been in before," they replied.

Soon they were swimming through a magnificent cave. Suddenly, a diver on a big black Aqua-Zepp underwater scooter roared up from behind them, hooked on to their line and shot off ahead into the system.

The cave divers went back to St Peter to complain that they were not the first into the cave. "Who was that guy with the big black Aqua-Zepp?" they asked. "Was it God?"

"No," replied St Peter. "That's Rob Palmer. He only thinks he's God."

It says something about Rob that he used to repeat that story with pride. As one of the best-known cave divers in the world at that time, with well-documented expeditions to explore Wookey Hole in the UK and the blue holes of the Bahamas, he understood that he was bound to attract envy in some quarters. Lesser divers were quick to criticise and he always appeared to relish it.

If Rob was unjustly regarded as arrogant by some, he could certainly take himself a bit seriously at times.

Rob wrote books and articles about organising expeditions. Those who went on his expeditions knew that as an expedition organiser, he was often totally disorganised. He was, however, an exemplary diver. He was knowledgeable, disciplined, avoided risks and was always cool under pressure.

An excellent teacher, he never missed a chance to pass on his knowledge. Many believed that to dive with him was to dive in as much safety as was possible. If he had a fault, it was that he could be a little bit earnest!

In May 1997 he was due to spend two weeks together with friends in the Red Sea. Rob was on good form despite losing all his luggage en-route from the Bahamas. Nothing ever seemed to faze him.

Week one was on the recently launched diving liveaboard MV *Moon Dancer*, at that time a new liveaboard venture in the Red Sea. Rob found time to conduct a semi-closed-circuit rebreather course and certified one lucky lady. It was to be the last certification he ever issued.

The second week was set aside for the first international conference of the technical diving agency TDI (Middle East) in Hurghada and the delegates started their week with a morning trip out on a day boat to dive a coral reef and to put them in the mood. Back on shore, Bret Gilliam, then President of TDI, soon heard the news that had come through on the dive centre's radio that Rob had failed to return from his dive. Bret was clearly shocked.

Others, sadly, were not. It was the culmination of something that had been half-expected to happen during the previous seven days.

Bret met the dive boat as it returned and tied up at the jetty. All on board were suffering from a mixture of shock and disbelief. Bret talked to those who had been in the water with Rob, including Tim, the teenage diver who had partnered him the previous week.

A factual, carefully worded release was submitted for publication through the Press Association. It was not the place for speculation.

Those who were there, later watched bemused, as respected newspapers concocted their own sensational explanations for the incident.

Rob had not been using a "secret rebreather", or been "trapped in a black hole" as reported by some, but those close to him believed he had been trapped, though not in any physical sense. He was trapped by his own state of mind.

A year before, Rob had been present when some American divers appeared to have undertaken an unnecessarily risky dive using ordinary air. This was later the subject of litigation when a magazine reported the story and the divers seemingly closed ranks. Although present at the time, Rob was neither part of the dive nor the apparent "cover-up". However, in a strange way some close friends sensed that he felt diminished by being excluded from the conspiracy. Some of those risky divers were likely to be arriving in Hurghada for the conference.

Those on board *Moon Dancer* had been promised an enjoyable series of dives on wrecks and coral reefs during the week's cruise. However, when Rob suggested they do some "deepies" there were few takers. Rob eventually teamed up with Tim, a young but seemingly sensible and intelligent diver. Tim and Rob both went into the water each armed with a twinset of air and a sling-tank of 50 per cent oxygen for use in decompression.

The reef walls of the northern Red Sea are incredibly deep. An extension of the African Rift Valley, the sea itself was formed by tectonic movements many eons ago. The coral grows in the shallows but there is the option for the scuba diver to drop almost as deep as they want subject only to the physiological limitations.

Later during that dive some of the others noticed the pair doing a decompression stop at a far greater depth than might have been considered normal. Back on board *Moon Dancer*, one took a casual look at Rob's computer. A chill ran through him when he realised he had read a maximum depth of 120 m (390 ft). Rob was tackled about it later in private, but to no effect.

Air is mainly composed of two gases, nitrogen and oxygen. Both these gases are associated with problems for life support when breathed under the pressure of extreme depth. Nitrogen has a narcotic effect whereas oxygen at high pressures can be fatally toxic. For that reason, air is not the appropriate gas to breathe at extreme depths.

Rob had always been a great champion and pioneer of technical diving. He advocated rich nitrox mixes for shallow water decompression and was an enthusiastic exponent of trimix (a gas mix using helium and thereby reducing the amount of oxygen and nitrogen) for use at depth. He pursued increased safety by reducing the amount of offensive gas in the breathing mix. "But get it wrong and you're dead!" he would say. He also coined the phrase, "A good attitude keeps you alive."

Yet here he was throwing everything he believed to the wind – breathing ordinary air at extreme depths and subjecting his body to a dive with an exceedingly high level of oxygen content that was getting on for twice the safe limit for oxygen toxicity. There was no other aim than to experience the lure of deep water itself.

His companions were confused and appalled. They had always enjoyed the way Rob not only shared his skills, but was also open-minded about others' ideas. It hurt to find their mentor acting so far out of character. Surely, this had to be a temporary aberration?

As Rob repeated these deep dives using plain air throughout the latter part of the week, exchanges between his closest friends in his cabin became more and more heated. When he expressed the mind-boggling opinion that it was safe to use air to 130 m (427 ft) deep, he did so in private. However, he was later heard discussing with other passengers "the cosy effect of narcosis as it closes around him". He was referring to the well-documented narcotic effect of breathing the inert nitrogen in air under the pressure of depth.

Eventually only the vessel's official dive guide, Sarah, seemed oblivious to what was going on. She daily recommended a depth limit of 30 m (100 ft) in her dive briefings. The general feeling on board was that what Rob did was his own business. By the end of the week most were intrigued not so much by whether there would be a fatality as by what he was trying to prove.

Knowledge is power and when you share that knowledge you must share the power. Once Rob had taught people what he knew, they would go off and become experts in their own right. Some even seemed to regard their former teacher as a threat. He had fallen out with several old associates, probably for that reason.

It's one thing to get famous, another to stay there. Continuing renown was one thing Rob really seemed to crave. It can only be concluded that, like an old gunslinger, he felt threatened by younger and newer people on the scene, as well as by the riskier and, in some cases, notorious exploits of certain of his peers.

Whoever you are, you must obey the natural laws and Rob chose to test what he had been teaching about oxygen toxicity. He repeatedly subjected his body to exceedingly high levels of oxygen. Rob was killed by physics. As he always told every diver he met, you get away with it until you don't. It was an ill-founded competitive streak and possibly a mid-life crisis that was his Achilles heel.

Repeated dives in excess of 100 m (325 ft) breathing compressed air killed Rob Palmer, but we can never be sure what was going on in his mind. On that final day, he entered the water with Tim, two other young men, Jean-Michel and Mila, and a young woman called Jane. Rob was twice the age of some of them. He was their role model.

The scene was a typical deep-water reef in the Giftun Islands outside Hurghada. It was Jane who, during the descent, decided to stop at 70 m (228 ft). Tim and Jean-Michel reported they stopped at 107 m (348 ft), while Mila appears to have gone off on a dive of his own. Rob was last seen below the others, at great depth, apparently waving them to continue on down.

Tim said afterwards when the boat docked: "He's lost. He's not coming back. He just kept swimming on down."

There was to be no other achievement other than the lure of depth itself. As Karim Helal, organiser of the TDI conference, said at the time, "Whoever you are, you can't beat the physics."

IN SEARCH OF
FREE-DIVING RECORDS

There's nothing free in diving and in the pursuit of free-diving records, free-divers sometimes risk their lives.

I t was Chris Boardman, the world champion cyclist, Olympic gold medallist, Blue Ribbon holder and an accomplished scuba diver, who observed that any sport that meant putting your life on the line as a matter of intent, had something seriously wrong with it. That is what free-divers do. They try to get as deep as possible after a single inhalation of air. If they go too far, they die.

Free-diving records go back to Frenchman Jacques Mayol and Sicilian Enzo Maiorca. Mayol first broke the 100 m (325 ft) barrier for a dive successfully completed on one breath taken at the surface. That record stood for so long that Mayol felt he owned it. Luc Besson made a film about it starring Jean Reno and Jean-Marc Barr called *The Big Blue*. It was also translated into Besson's native French and achieved cult status among movie buffs as *Le Grand Bleu*.

The story of the film concerned a couple of diving friends that performed rescues and otherwise speared fish in the Mediterranean, an area that has a long tradition of breath-hold divers fishing with spear guns. Enzo Maiorca's name in the film was changed to Enzo Molinari.

However, Italian moviegoers were denied the right to see this film after Enzo Maiorca successfully took legal action against its showing. In the climax to the story he dies while under water. In real life, Jacques Mayol went on to enjoy a lucrative career as an after-dinner speaker before committing suicide, whereas Enzo might have been forgotten by the free-diving world, but simply preferred to outlive his old rival to a fulfilled old age.

Since then, the sport of breath-hold diving has developed far beyond the straightforward requirement to stalk and kill fishes. People started finding different ways to do more than simply swim down armed with fins, mask and snorkel. At the present time, the governing body of the sport, AIDA, breaks up the different ways of achieving the goal, or disciplines, by the method used. This can be as simple as diving down unaided or by one of many other methods. Those that have gone deepest have commonly used a weighted sled that hurtles down a fixed line. It's called the No-Limits category.

Once at their predetermined target depth, the diver picks off a marked tag as proof they got there and then hurtles equally quickly back to the surface by means of a bag or balloon inflated from an air cylinder attached to the sled. One might liken it to a reverse parachute. The greatest challenge for the participants is to be able to equalise the extremely fast pressure changes in their ears. They usually don't wear a mask.

In the early nineties, the record for the greatest depth was shared alternately between two men: gentlemanly Umberto Pelizarri from Italy and Cuban-American Jose Ferreras, otherwise known as Pipin. Each regularly squeezed down another metre to add to the record depth.

The rivalry between these two became so intense that when it came to filming a remake of *Le Grand Bleu*, entitled *Ocean Men: Extreme Dive*, starring both protagonists, the two refused to speak to each other or even be on the same boat together during filming. Doubles were used for those crucial scenes where they are shown together. Eventually, Pipin managed a record descent to a depth of 160 m (524 ft) deeper than Pelizarri's maximum of 150 m (492 ft).

Since that time, numerous other people, including notably, a lovely English girl called Tanya Streeter, have extended the depth to which they were prepared to risk their lives. At one time, she held or equalled virtually all the records, including even those for men, with a No-Limits record of 160 m (525 ft), a feat that was quite remarkable.

It is the nature of records that they are there to be broken. Since Tanya's more recent dominance of the record books all manner of people have come forward to extend the depth in all of the various categories. Austrian Herbert Nitsch beat his own No-Limits free-diving record to set a new world record at an astounding depth of 214 m (699 ft) in 2011. He used a novel technique of pre-flooding his sinuses to cope with the pressure changes.

Alas, it's not a sport that appeals to spectators and no riches are there to be earned from success, nor do the successful become household names. David Avallone, from Cressisub, the Italian company that sponsored Umberto Pelizarri for many years, admitted that few people outside the world of diving had heard of him, and often questioned the commercial value of the company's association with him.

So people risk their lives for not much remuneration, although Tanya is now pursuing a film career. Some have not made it back from depth. Some have even become fatalities while practising holding their breath in their baths.

Of all the deaths that have resulted from these attempts to be the deepest person to dive on one breath and return safely to the surface, the tragic story of Audrey Mestre must be the most poignant.

Audrey was beautiful, young and French. She became hooked on the sport as a teenager and felt that she could learn more from a master of the art. She beat a path to Pipin's door. Pipin, ever the showman and not known for his modest ego, found it an asset to have such an attractive young woman on his arm. Before long romance blossomed and they were married. Under his tutelage, she managed to progress down to greater and greater depths.

Eventually, she was ready to make an attempt on a No-Limits record that might have exceeded Pipin's own. The Dominican Republic was chosen as the location for the attempt. Carlos Serra, Pipin's erstwhile business manager and now his former partner, was so upset by what happened during their time preparing for the attempt and its aftermath, that he wrote a book exposing the sequence of events from his point of view. It was called *The Last Attempt*.

If what he wrote was true, it is shocking to say the least. Sadly, the laws of libel are such that those that reviewed the book in magazines, were very limited in how they could describe its content. To repeat a libel can be construed as making the libel itself and reviewers shied away from that. Suffice to say the book seems to have sunk without trace, which is more than can be said for Audrey Mestre. Her body was brought back.

What we do know is that, during the record attempt, she achieved the target depth but found that her sled's air cylinder was crucially empty at the moment she came to inflate the bag that was intended to send her back safely to the surface.

Carlos Serra alleges that Pipin seemed to have been able to anticipate this. It was Pipin who was thought to be responsible for ensuring her air cylinder was filled to the maximum pressure. Sublime as a free-diver, Pipin is said to have surprised everyone on board the support boat that day, by taking a scuba set and swimming down ostensibly to meet his wife, but it was to where one of the support divers (on scuba) was already attempting to retrieve Audrey's lifeless body. Unable to reach the surface under her own power, she'd simply drowned at depth and her body was not recovered until nine minutes into her record attempt.

The world will never get to know what happened. The police in the Dominican Republic chose not to investigate even though Carlos Serra alleged a crime was committed. Audrey Mestre might well have been a victim of overconfidence on the part of both her and her husband. The story attracted the attention of film-maker James Cameron.

A year after her death, Ferreras (Pipin) completed a No-Limits dive to match Mestre's depth of 171 m (561 ft), the depth from which she failed to return alive. Pipin appears since to have left the free-diving record attempt scene to younger people. We'll never know but free-diving records continue to be broken and so too the bodies of some of those that find their chosen target depth to be a depth too far.

PART NINE

Treasure Seekers and Finders

PIN MONEY AND
KING HENRY VIII

An unnamed diver earns a little pin money when he finds some Tudor treasure in the Thames.

When it came to women, King Henry VIII was known as a bit of a dog. His recorded marriages and the consequences for his brides are well known. "Divorced, beheaded, died, divorced, beheaded, survived" is a quick way of remembering the sequence. What is less appreciated is that in those times, it was quite normal for gentlemen to keep concubines, ladies used for sexual favours, and this was generally known as "being kept under the protection" of the nobleman concerned.

King Henry VIII said he knew what women wanted. They wanted their own way. That said, as the all-powerful monarch, some would say tyrant, he was not known entirely for his altruism. No doubt he had his own succession of lady friends that he had ensconced in various stately houses.

In Tudor times, the main thoroughfare of London was the river Thames. Travel by road at that time tended to be very uncomfortable if not dangerous. All the mighty houses were built along the banks of the Thames from beyond Greenwich and Tilbury in the east, past Tide End Town, now known as Teddington, virtually all the way to Windsor and what is now Reading in the west. One of the most magnificent was Hampton Court Palace, then a country house, which the king sequestered from his chancellor, Wolsey, in order to make a convenient home for his intended second wife, the unfortunate Anne Boleyn. You can still see and visit the palace standing in all its medieval glory today.

Of course, many of the lesser Tudor houses have long gone, but these villas overlooking the water of the river gave gentlemen a discreet access by boat to visit their lady friends. Their lady friends, no doubt, usually hoped that these relationships might develop into something more permanent.

On the other hand, the gentlemen would keep their mistresses distracted with generous gifts that were usually in the form of jewellery. Jewelled rings had too much of a legitimising significance so gentlemen favoured broaches and gold pins that could be worn in the hair.

When the relationship came to its inevitable end, as anyone would know it was destined to do when the gentleman found a new and younger paramour, the previous lady was ruined. Evicted from her former home, often all she had to fall back on to support her were the jewellery or pins she might have kept. The money this raised when sold was known as "pin money", hence the origin of the term.

The break-up of a relationship can be traumatic. Tempers can get frayed and tantrums ensue. One such young woman foolishly decided to throw all the gifts that her lover had bestowed upon her out of a window of the house and down into the river below.

More than 450 years later, a diver searching around in the mud of the river Thames, close by the location of a former Tudor villa, struck lucky. He had been hoping to find the odd post-medieval artefact, some item that might have fallen in the water while being transferred from boat to shore, a candlestick, the remains of a musket, maybe a religious cross discarded at the reformation of the monasteries, but he found more.

In England there are laws regarding the finding of treasure. It's known as "Treasure Trove". It is applied where the treasure seems old enough for it to be presumed that the true owner is dead and the heirs undiscoverable.

A new law, incorporated in the Coroner's and Justice Bill 2009, now makes it a legal duty of those in possession of any item that is or might be treasure, to report it to the authorities within 14 days of acquiring it or becoming aware that it could be treasure. It is then subject to tax.

For that reason what follows next could be hearsay.

Richard and Mark were brothers. They were brothers who lived near the river and had recently taken up scuba diving. They were very keen on their new hobby but were frustrated that once again the weather on the coast had let them down and their planned club dive was cancelled. They decided to rig their shiny new diving equipment and take it for a spin in the river.

They were disappointed to find that the water was not as deep as they had expected. In some places they had trouble getting both themselves and their tanks submerged and, although it looked clear enough from the bank, the visibility at the water's edge was almost zero.

Mark had suggested they dived under and around a nearby bridge. People were always throwing things off he reasoned, but Richard had other ideas. He persuaded his brother to carry his diving equipment with him along the towpath to near where an old wall of a big house stood. He reasoned that rich people who might have owned a boat and moored it there, would have dropped stuff accidentally in the water. Maybe they'd get lucky and find a Rolex.

Their diving equipment attracted the attention of an elderly gentleman riding a bicycle. Divers are quite uncommon on the banks of the Thames, especially in the higher reaches. He asked them what they were intending to dive on. Was it a lost cabin cruiser? Mark reluctantly admitted that it was nothing as exciting as that. They were just going in to see what was there. The old man said in that case they should walk a little further along the path to where the wall stopped. He said it had been the site of a Tudor house that had burnt down and fallen in the river. They might well find something interesting nearby. Maybe they'd find some real treasure. That is how they came to be wallowing around in the shallow water near the bank and grovelling in the mud.

There's a lot of commitment to diving. By the time they had transported their equipment, rigged it, got into their suits and struggled down the bank into the water, they were determined to make the most of it. Not only that, but sliding down the riverbank had made a few bad grass stains on their expensive new drysuits.

It wasn't easy. The water flowed on endlessly as rivers do, and although it promised to make the work harder, it actually helped by washing the released mud away from them as they made their way upstream.

Each time one of them felt a solid object, they would break the surface and examine it. It was amazing how much rubbish they came across, but they eventually found a few silver forks and spoons as a reward for their efforts. They had given up any dreams of finding anything as fanciful as a lost gold chalice or suchlike.

It was towards the end of the afternoon, with both the summer sunshine and their enthusiasm waning, that Richard, fed up with working in mud, made his way out into a deeper, clearer part of the river.

As he wafted away the silt of the riverbed, a mass of gold objects suddenly appeared, twinkling in the evening light. There seemed to be dozens of them.

He could hardly believe his eyes and collected what he could. It was the mother lode. It was almost as easy as picking coins up from the bottom of the Trevi fountain. They turned out to be ornately engraved solid gold pins of different lengths and from the Tudor period.

There were more than he could carry. It wasn't disclosed how many of these items he retrieved or what happened to them afterwards. Neither Richard nor Mark is telling, but suffice to say that Richard was seen soon after driving a new car.

BLUE HOLE DIVING

Primeval caves that have since flooded, provide a remarkable diving experience but it is not for everyone.

S teffi Schwabe strode ahead of Brendan through the swampland, shrugging off attacks by aggressive insects as easily as she carried her two steel diving cylinders, swinging from her hips. It was mid-summer and the Bahamas were enjoying particularly hot and humid weather.

Brendan followed pathetically behind, a deafening pulse in his head and sweat from his forehead stinging his eyes.

"Blue holes are the entrances into some of the world's most spectacular cave systems," she told him. "These openings can be found among the shallow creeks, inland lakes and shallow banks of the Bahamas."

For many years, popular ideas about the origin of blue holes have been mixed with local superstition and myth. Cenote-type caves can be found both inland and in a marine setting.

Water movement is generally restricted in these systems and in many instances several distinct thermoclines, haloclines and chemoclines can be found within the water column. The Lucayan caverns are part of the most extensive cave system known to exist in Grand Bahama, with more than 10 km (6 miles) of mapped passages.

There are three known dry and two wet entrances to the system. The latter discharge into a mangrove creek, and the main dry entrance is known as Ben's Cave, named after Ben Rose, a long time instructor who first explored these caves.

During Brendan's visit with Steffi, Ben's Cave was closed to protect the vast number of bats that were roosting there. These bats provide an important source of nutrients to the waters in the form of guano, while feeding the mangrove snapper with the occasional baby bat that falls into the water.

Following a line, Steffi took Brendan to the Lucayan Burial Mound entrance – named after an Indian burial mound found at the site – which was also home to plenty of roosting bats. Brendan considered them important allies in his ongoing war against the constant swarm of mosquitoes and horse flies that attacked him. He didn't care that his equipment had to be put down on a surface of thick bat excrement.

"I really enjoy taking people into these caves, to share what I experience so often. I like to see their reactions," Steffi enthused.

After the exhausting walk, carrying his camera gear and diving equipment through the undergrowth to the cave, it was a relief to get into the cool of the open cave and have a swim in the freshwater pool. Kitted out with adequate air supplies and lights, they dropped down through the pool to 14 m (45 ft) deep where a sign indicated that it was prohibited to enter the cave.

Steffi had special permission because she was doing research, and Brendan was allowed to accompany her to take some photographs.

They entered the flooded outer chamber, which was enormous – about the size of a small church. This part of the cavern was about 10 m (33 ft) deep, except for some parts where old collapses had left rock piles, leaving them in only 5 m (16 ft) of water.

Tree roots hung down around them and in one corner they could see the light streaming in through another entrance, silhouetting more tree roots. This was made even more dramatic by a tropical storm that had broken since they left the fresh air above, creating random blue shafts of light that flashed with the lightning. Hammer House of Horror meets Jean-Michel Jarre!

This area was called the Skylight Room. Some say it is possible to snorkel the 100 m (328 ft) from the entrance to this hole where water meets air, but it would be unwise to try! This is real cave diving, to be given the respect it demands.

In one corner, at least 50 m (160 ft) from the nearest entrance, lies an old black rubber fin. Steffi later told Brendan that it had been there since before the cave was first officially dived. One could imagine the panic of some itinerant snorkeller lost in that dark place, losing a fin in the mad scramble to find the way out.

Naturally, they had the benefit of a previously laid guide-line, but in such a vast space it was easy to lose sight of the thin white cord if you ventured far from it without clipping on your own line first. The line carried little metal direction arrows to the exit to avoid confusion.

Leaving this first chamber, they set off downwards through the strong halocline. At one point it became impossible to see because of the intermingling of fresh and salt water. The original guide-line had become broken at this point so Steffi went on ahead to replace it.

Once she had moved more than a few metres from him, Brendan could still see her lights but it was impossible to focus his eyes on her. With the line safely tied off, she came back and escorted him onwards. As she led the way, he noticed how her fin tips were making the water go "wibbly-wobbly".

This soon increased to the point where his vision was so disturbed that his mask almost became redundant. Brendan realised he could not see the guide-line even in the beams of his powerful lights.

At about 23 m (75 ft), the freshwater element of the mix was left behind and he regained perfect vision. Steffi searched for a previously laid experiment among the colourful mung on the cave floor. Mung is a word used to describe the bacterial detritus that lies 28 m (91 ft) down on the cave floor, and they needed to be careful how they used their fins. Stir up the mung and they'd soon be feeling their way back!

Finally, they ascended into the Wedding Hall Room. This was the treasure that they had come for. Stalactites and stalagmites untouched by human hand contrived a magnificent scene. It was a cathedral dressed in white marble. A wedding cake made of white candy icing. Everywhere they shone their lights revealed more of what few people had ever cast their eyes upon. It was a visual treasure.

Brendan got busy with his camera, its flash lighting up an architecture that had been formed in prehistoric times before sea levels rose and filled the cave. Film finished, he started to swim off in totally the wrong direction before coming to the next direction arrow attached to the guide-line. It pointed the other way and he learned a swift lesson in how easily one can get disorientated in these conditions.

"Lose the line and lose your life" is a cave diver's maxim. Most accidents in cave diving have been associated with the loss or absence of a properly laid guide-line, and in this case the attached direction arrows proved just how essential they were. At this point they were a couple of hundred metres from the entrance. Some professional cave divers have made record-breaking journeys into cave systems that have been more than 9 km (6 miles) from the safety of the entrance.

AN ARCHAEOLOGICAL FIND

Archaeology under water can be disappointing even when it's worthwhile.

I t was a trip shrouded in mystery from the beginning. Mike Braun had invited some friends to dive a Red Sea wreck site but there was a cloak of mystery surrounding the arrangements. He was unable or unwilling to give his guests much detail. He told them it might be something very exciting or it might be nothing. It would occupy a week of their time. Were they prepared to take the risk?

Air tickets duly arrived that took wreck hunter, the late Steve Carmichael-Timson, and a few other selected friends, to Hurghada. It was a long eight hours or so later, after passing Egyptian immigration officials, and with a less than comfortable drive, that they were met in darkness at a fly-blown jetty in southern Egypt and ferried over to where a luxurious motor yacht waited. That was to be home for the next week.

They set off southwards at a great lick on a waxy calm sea and travelled overnight to a place that was called Habili Saleh. It was around 48 km (30 miles) south of Dangerous Reef and very close to the border with the Sudan. Ahmed Fadel, the regular dive guide aboard the yacht, had dived the site before during an exploration trip, and had evidently stumbled across something interesting.

Crossing the top of the reef by inflatable, they dropped down on to a sandy-looking seabed dotted with small coral heads. First, there were two large anchors petrified yet strangely upright in the seabed. Another large item that they first mistook for a third anchor was later thought by Steve to be the metal parts of a rudder assembly of a very old boat. Then there was what looked very much like a ship's bell. All around there were the outlines of pottery showing up through the sand, but these seemed to be from a much earlier era. There were assorted amphorae, decorative urns and large jugs, strewn across an area of the seabed about the size of a football pitch at 23 m (75 ft) deep. In some cases the pottery looked quite sophisticated with square handles whereas others were simple conical-shaped storage jars.

The problem was that they were not simply lying there, waiting to be picked up by some itinerant diver. Lifting anything was out of the question, both legally and practically. Everything was well concreted into a rocky substrate that lay only a centimetre or so below a layer of sand. Was this a seriously important ancient wreck site?

One job was to photograph as many of the finds where they lay as possible, in order that the pictures could be shown to an expert who could make that judgement. Steve's contribution was to check the seabed for evidence of metal structures with his underwater metal detector and to survey the whole area with his side-scan sonar that, in conjunction with his laptop computer, could render a picture of what was down there. In this way he could cover an area that would have been impossible by a few scuba divers.

They dived to see what was worth closer attention, marking likely candidates for further attention with ping-pong balls on string. Steve got to work with his metal detector, spotting lots of interesting collections of readings that indicated a fair scattering of metal pieces. They found a few items that looked to them like copper nails.

Of course, they were each equally excited about the bell. It was a simple-looking shape but it was decided that if they could clean it up and photograph it, it might well reveal all the clues that were needed to know what was lying there.

It was completely concreted in, so they set to cleaning it off where it lay. This involved a great deal of hard work. The depth may not sound very much but if you want a lot of time down there, short decompression stops on the way back up are going to be a fact of life. They had to use their dive time carefully so they decided to work a rota, each diver doing 20 minutes of hard graft followed, by an ascent of 15 or so minutes. This dive profile allowed them to get in several dives each day.

Mike went in first and got to work. His girlfriend Cat was a hard working part of the team. When the next diver's time came to take over it was easy for him to spot Mike by the tremendous stream of bubbles exhaled from his regulator, such was the effort he was putting in. Meanwhile, Ahmed and Steve were busy setting up the side-scan sonar. By the next dive they were ready with a full complement of divers to work on the bell.

They soaked up plenty of nitrogen and expended a lot of effort until they came to do the last dive on the bell. Strict instructions were given that it should not be moved in any way from where it was at least until it had been photographed. Ahmed went in first this time and got to work, followed by Mike. The diver with the camera passed Ahmed doing a lengthy decompression stop as he dropped down, only to be met by Mike not working around the bell at all, but now starting on an amphora nearby. He motioned over to where the bell lay and it was clear that it now had a hole in it. It wasn't a bell at all. It was simply a bell-shaped terracotta pot. Mike's disappointment was palpable. He looked very despondent and signalled to the photographer that they should both ascend. As they swam towards the reef they saw several more "bells" that they simply hadn't noticed before. It's funny how the mind will play tricks especially if you are into wishful thinking.

Back onboard, an impromptu discussion resulted in the general disappointment being put to one side and the decision was made to choose some good examples of the amphorae and other pottery, clean them up where they lay to reveal them as best they could, and get them photographed. Some of the amphorae were disqualified from attention because they had coral growing on them.

The others went in first with wire brushes and chipping tools and Steve and the photographer followed later with video, still photography equipment and scale bars to lie alongside each item.

The water was thick with sand and detritus that had been liberated by those doing the hard work, but the job was quickly accomplished; the pictures were duly digitally processed and sent off to the various experts around the world for some informed assessment.

Ross Iain Thomas of Southampton University, later examining the pictures resulting from the project for *Diver* magazine, said this:

"A number of interesting features can be found on this Red Sea mystery wreck that help identify its purpose and date. Firstly traces of the superstructure are preserved in the form of copper alloy nails and lead sheathing from either the bow or stern end. Lead sheathing was constructed from large sheets 1–2 mm thick that were laid over pitch waterproofing and held in place by copper tacks hammered into the wooden hull. This was used to protect the hull from marine borers that would damage the hull and is attested on the hulls of fifth century BC to second century AD wrecks in the Mediterranean (Parker 1992: 199). Lead sheeting and copper tacks fitting this description have been found in first century BC through to third century AD deposits in the Red Sea Roman ports of Myos Hormos (Peacock et al.) and Berenike (Sidebotham et al.), where no doubt vessels like this would have anchored and been maintained.

At least two ancient iron anchors can be seen on the photographs. Two armed stock iron anchors occur in the Mediterranean from the Roman Republican period onwards, though the curved arms of these examples are typical of the Early Imperial Roman period (Kapitan 1984: 42). Both the hull and anchors suggest this vessel was built in the traditional Mediterranean fashion. Its presence in the Red Sea is unsurprising as Rome controlled much of the Red Sea coast after its annexation of Egypt in 30 BC and Nabataea (modern Jordan) in 106 AD. Greco-Roman merchants took this opportunity to be involved in the Red Sea and Indian Ocean trade of exotic spices and incense with South Arabia, East Africa and India.

The vessel was clearly a merchant vessel as represented by the numerous cargo amphorae found at the site. Though detailed analysis of these amphorae would greatly increase our understanding of the vessels, some observations can be made from the photos. Firstly the amphorae are easily recognised from the bifid handles, bead rim, long cylindrical body and short spike. These were produced in a variety of locations including Italy, Spain, Greece, Turkey, France, Tunisia and Egypt from the late first century BC to the early or mid-third century AD. Broad, long Egyptian amphorae ending in a solid spike with two small looped handles at or just under the rim can also be identified. These were produced in Egypt from the first century BC through to fifth century AD. Lastly a squat form with a flat ring base, short flaring neck with a beaded rim was also found. These were produced in France and Spain, though similar forms were also produced in North Africa from AD 50 to the end of the third century AD.

These three amphora forms were specifically used to transport wine and it is likely that this wreck was on its way to Arabia, East Africa or India to trade wine for spices, incense or other high value and exotic goods demanded by the wealthy Roman public. In combination the amphorae, hull sheathing and anchors all suggest that this Roman merchant ship wrecked at some point between the second half of the first century AD and the beginning of the third century AD on its way from Berenike (Port Berenice) to an unknown destination in the Red Sea or Indian Ocean."

Alas, it seems that the appropriate authorities in Egypt have no immediate interest in this wreck site. There are, at the time of writing, no plans for further investigation by experts. From time to time, leisure divers based on liveaboard boats, still visit the site and in line with current local regulations: nothing may be disturbed or brought back to the surface, nor should any of the coral growing on artifacts be damaged. It appears that it must lie there undisturbed for a further period of time, if not for another 2000 years, before it catches the interest of marine archeologists.

EL BAJO AND THE LOST
VIDEO CAMERA

Losing an expensive toy off the side of a boat into deep water can ruin your day, but if you're lucky someone will be waiting to help.

Unlike ordinary scuba gear, closed-circuit rebreathers (CCRs) can automatically adjust to give the diver the most optimum gas mix at any given depth, maximising the time allowed at depth while minimising the time required to make the ascent. At the same time, because a diver rebreathing uses only the oxygen he actually metabolises, while the carbon dioxide he produces as a by-product is chemically removed, gas use is at a minimum too. So, in effect, the diver can go deeper for longer with a CCR.

Although pure oxygen rebreathers have been around for a very long time indeed, especially for covert use by the military, they are depth limited. Peter Readey was an early pioneer of electronically controlled rebreathers suitable for use by leisure divers and produced a pioneering item of CCR equipment called the Prism. Like most of today's leisure CCRs, it automatically mixed the breathing gas to give the optimum percentage of oxygen at any particular depth.

It was still early days in the development when he met up with three other rebreather divers at La Paz, Baja California Sur, in Mexico. One was La Paz resident Luke Inman while the other two were simply there to use their prototype Prisms, and what better than to do it in the company of the inventor?

They called themselves the Three Musketeers. We can only guess that young Luke was d'Artagnan.

Near La Paz, in the Sea of Cortez, lies a very famous dive site called El Bajo. It's a deep seamount and in the past has become famous for the schooling hammerhead sharks attracted to it. It's probably the most famous dive site in the Sea of Cortez.

Because of its depth, ordinary scuba divers tend to be limited for time there. Taking your chances at seeing sharks in a short window of opportunity can be subject to disappointment. These four rebreather divers would be able to use their closed-circuit equipment to best advantage and they set off to dive there.

At the same time another group of ordinary leisure divers were getting ready to depart for El Bajo, but when the rebreather divers first arrived, theirs was the only boat.

They prepared their kit and got into the water, descending quickly the 30 m (100 ft) to the top of the seamount. They were disappointed to find there was no sign of any pelagic animals. So they set off to the bottom of the seamount, which was at around twice the depth of the top.

The four of them swam along, checking that their rebreathers were operating correctly, but if they were honest they would probably say that they were a little bored. There was very little to catch the eye and they were down there for about 40 minutes before a bright object lying on the seabed came to their notice.

It was a brand new Top Dawg underwater video housing, just lying there on the rocky substrate all shiny and silver. You can imagine there was a bit of a rush and a tussle as the four rebreather divers wrestled over ownership of this prized find.

Eventually, one of them took charge of it and it was time to ascend.

At this point, it was noted that one of their number had come equipped with a diving computer only suitable for ordinary open-circuit scuba diving. While the others knew that they could come to the surface in reasonably short order, this guy insisted on coming up at the ascent rate mandated by his computer and doing all the pauses for decompression required on the way. As he was the one holding on to the newly found video camera housing, the other three felt compelled to stay with him.

Without the advantages of a decompression schedule suitable for use with a closed-circuit rebreather, the ascent took more than an hour during which time they were buzzed by a marlin, probably the most exciting part of the dive.

The four hung below a surface-marker buoy so that their boat could follow them and pick them safely up when they surfaced. During the hour, on the gentle ocean current, they probably covered a couple of miles and were out of sight of where they had started when they broke the surface.

Finally, they reached fresh air and the self-imposed silence was broken as they bobbed in the water, discussing who was to be the owner of their treasure.

The boat picked them up and they climbed on board, chattering excitedly. One wondered how much money he would get for the video housing while another wanted to know if it had a camera inside. It did.

"Look, this housing doesn't have any growth on it. It looks brand new. It can only have been in the sea for a very short time," suggested Luke. They unclipped the back of the housing and took the camcorder out. It was the latest model.

"Let's go back to the El Bajo dive site in case there is another dive boat there that arrived after we went into the water."

Their crew confirmed another boat had just pulled up as they submerged.

"We'll have to go back and ask them if they lost it."

In the meantime, one of the other divers was looking at the video that was stored in the camcorder. None of it was under water. They set off back.

The sea was calm as glass and another small dive boat floated aimlessly over El Bajo.

"Have you lost anything?" Luke shouted to a man on the deck.

"You'll never find it. We've been looking for hours," he shouted back despondently.

"Was it a Top Dawg video housing?" Luke persisted.

"Yes, but you won't find it, even with those rebreathers. We've been searching forever."

"Did it have a Sony TR camcorder inside it?"

"Yes but I've already told you that we've searched for hours."

By now the other man was getting irritated by all these questions. His day was ruined if not his whole trip. He could do without the cross-examination.

"How did you lose it?"

"It simply got knocked off the deck into the water," he replied downcast. He'd got used to the idea he'd lost his precious new toy. It was gone forever. By now the four rebreather divers were beginning to enjoy watching his ongoing pain.

"Did the camcorder have Radio Shack batteries in it?"

There comes a moment in a man's life when he reaches an epiphany, an enlightenment. This was such a moment. Luke and the other three rebreather divers watched the man's face as it changed from complete despair to the realisation that there might be hope at last.

"How could you have known about the batteries?" he asked thoughtfully.

At this point the shiny new video housing complete with its top-of-the-range camcorder safe inside was revealed. It's good in times of trouble to have d'Artagnan and the Three Musketeers to help.

REAL TREASURE

One of the most popular questions asked by non-divers of those that go under water is whether they ever found any treasure.

There is a frequently held misconception that every ship that makes passage across the ocean is loaded with bullion or that the captain's safe is stuffed with cash. People don't realise that it is the job of the ship's agent to supply any cash required for port costs or crew wages when the vessel docks. However, the dream persists and it's a dream believed in by many divers.

People do find treasure, but it's not easy. Mel Fisher spent most of his life searching before he found the wreck of the Spanish treasure ship the *Nuestra Señora de Atocha* off the Florida Keys and untold riches were recovered. That's not counting the riches taken when a thief stole one of the gold bars that was later on display in the Mel Fisher museum in Key West.

Fisher knew that a fleet of treasure ships had sunk off Florida in 1715 but it took him and his crew 16 years before they found success. In 1985 they stumbled across a quarter of a million valuable artefacts, coins and gold bars with an estimated value of more than half-a-billion US dollars.

REAL TREASURE

The HMS *Edinburgh* was sunk in 1941 in the Barents Sea while transporting Russian gold bullion from Murmansk to help pay for war supplies. Much of that gold was later discovered and recovered by Yorkshireman Keith Jessop and his divers. It was valued at more than one hundred million US dollars.

The so-called Nanking Treasure was composed of porcelain that had been transported along with a cargo of tea (the more valuable part of the cargo at the time) and this was recovered only after a lot of preparation. It was found in the wreck of a Dutch East Indiaman, the *Geldermalsen*, in 1981 and the porcelain was later sold at Christie's in Amsterdam. Its sale raised millions of Dutch guilders.

The same treasure hunter, Michael Hatcher, also discovered the wreck of the *Tek Sing* in 1999 and salvaged 350 000 pieces of Chinese porcelain that were auctioned in Germany in 2000 for 22.4 million Deutschmarks.

However, the diver's dream of the safe containing bullion on every ship that sinks continues, and it was noted that the first item even Jacques Cousteau lifted on visiting the wreck of the *Thistlegorm* in the 1950s, was the captain's safe. It is not recorded what was in it.

Sean McCabe, a commercial diver who often works at the underwater studio in Pinewood, the location of many scenes from films like *Pirates of the Caribbean*, heard about a safe that had fallen through the wooden planking of the pier at Southend-on-Sea in Essex. This was said to be the world's longest pleasure pier but it caught fire in 2005 and the safe had been lost when it fell through the burning floorboards into the water below. A pal of Sean's had recently discovered a small safe in the river Thames near London Airport and it had turned out to be "stuffed full" with American dollars. Dollar signs rolled in Sean's eyes once he got the salvage rights to the Southend Pier safe.

Sean hired massive lifting bags to raise the safe to the surface and an expensive crane to lift it from there. It proved to be a difficult and expensive job. When the safe was opened, it contained only £14 and some loose change to which Sean had the rights of 50 per cent.

Treasure doesn't have to be in precious metals, jewellery or cash though. Two diving instructors stocked the shop of their fledgling dive school with second-hand equipment by searching the bottom of an inland lake that was popular with divers who went there to practise techniques. They made it a point to visit early every Monday morning and regularly found many lost items, as did a diving instructor in Mallorca who went regularly to dive a remote bay that was a popular weekend haunt of rich boat owners. He found Raybans, an expensive Blancpain watch, towels, champagne glasses and notably, a Johnson 50 hp outboard motor that started on first pull once it was recovered to dry land. Other divers used to regularly search the shallow waters of the beaches in the Balearics with metal detectors and made a good living from selling the lost jewellery they found, that is until the authorities put a stop to it.

Commercial divers working in Scotland were surveying a stone pier. It had been subject to severe floods during winter and a restaurant that was built upon the pier had been totally washed away. Their job was to survey the remaining structure and make sure that it was still safe. It should have taken a couple of days but the job took a lot longer.

That's because the divers discovered the entire contents of the restaurant's wine cellar and its liquor store waiting to be collected from the muddy bottom of the loch. Collecting up all the bottles that were in perfect condition apart from damage to their labels took a lot longer than the survey. I don't suppose that any of them were returned to their rightful owner, by then the insurance company that covered the risk.

An English dive guide, working out in Egypt, spent six years removing brass fittings from the wreck of the *Carnatic*, a nineteenth-century P&O steam sailing ship that sank at Sha'ab Abu Nuhas in the Red Sea. The vessel had been carrying in excess of a million dollars' worth of gold at the time, but it was salvaged soon after her sinking. He removed and raised portholes, brass lamps fitted with gimbals called angel lamps and even the brass compass binnacle; this latter treasure had to be left temporarily on the reef due to his running out of air and another British dive boat skipper took the opportunity to carry it on the final leg of its journey to the surface and to his own private collection of brass. However, despite this setback, he regularly shipped the stuff back to England where most of it is stored today in a garden shed.

The Egyptian authorities soon got wise to this once the local diving industry got properly under way and heavy penalties are imposed on anyone interfering with or removing artefacts, or even parts of coral reef, from anywhere in Egyptian waters.

Peter Collings discovered this when he was found carrying an empty nineteenth-century bottle from the *Carnatic*. Unfortunately for him, Collings was spotted by an Egyptian dive guide, who tried to take it from him and return it to the wreck. A dangerous underwater fight broke out. Peter later claimed he was merely moving the bottle to a safe hiding place so that nobody else would steal it. Doubly unfortunate for Mr Collings was the fact that the whole incident was recorded on video by another Egyptian dive guide, Khaled Katawi. Gamal Lamouny, owner of the boat from which both the Egyptian guides came, tried to have Collings arrested on a charge of attempted murder, but luckily for him nothing was done about it.

British war wrecks are often designated as war graves and protected. It is an offence to take anything from them. Leicestershire resident Duncan Keates found this out when he boasted on his Facebook page of a fancy porthole he had taken from the wreck of the HMS *Duke of Albany*, a Great War casualty. After a police investigation, he was found guilty at Kirkwall Sheriff Court and fined £1400. We don't know what happened to the rest of his group of 10 divers that were photographed posing in front of the dive boat *Jeane Elaine* with a huge pile of trophies, including several portholes and the maker's plate apparently liberated at the same time. No doubt they were subject to similar police scrutiny.

Alex Double came across an unidentified old wreck loaded with porcelain, or so he thought, while diving during a southern Red Sea trip to the waters of the Hanish Islands of the Yemen. A friend carried a couple of examples back to London for him to have them valued at Sotheby's. Alas, they turned out to be pristine examples of cheap chinaware typical of the early twentieth century and less than a hundred years old.

The best story of all, concerns a diver who wishes to remain anonymous for obvious reasons. He stumbled across the recent wreck of an expensive motor cruiser that nobody seemed to have reported. It is thought that it might have been used by people smuggling drugs from North Africa to Spain and had suffered severe damage in some sort of high-speed collision, possibly with the nearby rocks that broke the surface a hundred metres or so from the sheer cliffs that formed the coastline. He assumed that running without lights, a lone navigator might have lost concentration and hit the rocks at high speed in the darkness. There was no sign of any body but from the otherwise pristine condition of the wreck, events had occurred very soon before his discovery.

The solitary diver entered the smashed-up vessel as it lay on its side like some discarded toy and found a cupboard that was secured by a heavy padlock. Armed with the appropriate tools he broke the hinges that secured its door. It took many days to dry out the millions of Spanish pesetas he found in bundles stacked inside and a lot longer to exchange the notes in small amounts for the sterling equivalent back home in the UK.

The incidents of discovered treasure are few and far between and the legal risks can be considerable. I would suggest the best anyone can hope for is to stay safe and treasure the experience.

Other titles
you might be interested in...

Our *ULTIMATE* Series

Collections of 100 extraordinary experiences
illustrated with striking full page photography

Diving   Surfing   Canoe & Kayak   Fishing   Skiing

The other titles in our *AMAZING* Series

All available from **www.fernhurstbooks.com**

Visit our website to discover our full range of titles and all that we have to offer.
Here you can also register to receive news, details of new books and
exclusive special offers.

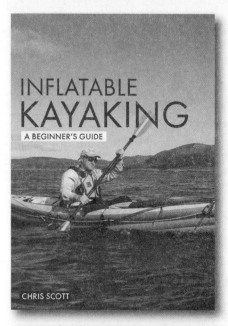
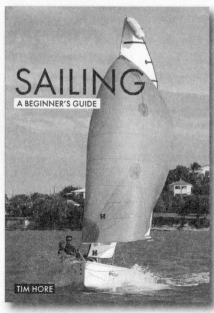
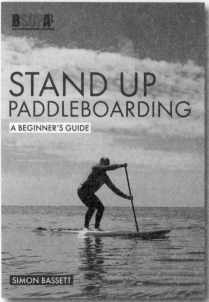
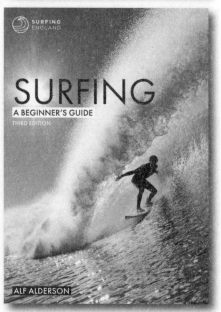

Tales of diving with the bizzare and the beautiful

Diving veteran **John Bantin** recounts many tales of his diving with several species of sharks & other marine animals over the last 4 decades.

Packed full of stunning underwater colour photography.

Find out more at www.fernhurstbooks.com

View our entire list at www.fernhurstbooks.com

•

Sign up to receive details of new books & exclusive special offers at
www.fernhurstbooks.com/register

•

Get to know us more on social media

FERNHURST BOOKS